Memory

Elizabeth Loftus

Memory

surprising new insights into how we remember and why we forget

Elizabeth Loftus

Addison-Wesley Publishing Company

Reading, Massachusetts
Menlo Park, California
London
Amsterdam
Don Mills, Ontario
Sydney

Library of Congress Cataloging in Publication Data

Loftus, Elizabeth F   1944-
  Memory, surprising new insights into how we
remember and why we forget.

  Includes index.
  1. Memory. I. Title. I
BF371.L635   153.1'2   80-18989
ISBN 0-201-04473-0
ISBN 0-201-04474-9 (pbk.)

ISBN 0-201-04473-0-H
      0-201-04474-9-P

ABCDEFGHIJ-DO-89876543210

To the memory of my mother, who died over twenty years ago, and to my Uncle Joe and Aunt Kitty, who continually helped me to keep that memory alive

Acknowledgments

I owe a great debt to the Stanford University Center for Advanced Studies in the Behavioral Sciences, where in the summer of 1979 I wrote the first draft of this book. Financial support from the Andrew W. Mellon Foundation and the National Science Foundation to the Center is gratefully acknowledged. The National Science Foundation also generously provided a portion of my salary during that time. Dr. James Fries, who really suggested that I write this book, deserves a great deal of thanks. Many other Fellows at the Center similarly inspired my idea. My husband and close friend, Geoffrey Loftus, stood by me through the thick and thin of revising. And finally, I thank the people at Addison-Wesley, especially Warren Stone, Doe Coover, Ann Dilworth, Brian Crockett, and Tess Palmer, for all the work they did to make this a better book.

Also by Elizabeth Loftus

Cognitive Processes
(with Lyle Bourne and
Roger Dominowski)

Eyewitness Testimony

Human Memory
(with Geoffrey Loftus)

Learning
(with Sarnoff Mednick and
Howard Pollio)

Contents

Introduction: The Memory Doctor

Memory is something we usually take for granted, but stop for a moment and imagine life without it. Every day we would have to learn everything all over again. We would wake up in the morning, discover the kitchen, find the coffee pot, then the shower. We would have to figure out anew how to get dressed, cook scrambled eggs and toast, drive a car. Life would be a never-ending discovery, exhausting us before we had lasted a single week.

Do memories last forever? Many people believe that everything we learn is permanently stored in the mind, even though particular details may not be immediately accessible. With hypnosis or other special techniques, these inaccessible details could eventually be recovered. As we shall see, this belief is now being seriously challenged. New studies suggest that our memories are continually being altered, transformed, and distorted. After nearly a century of experimental research, psychologists are beginning to discover a great deal about this and other aspects of mental life. The work advances at a snail's pace, however, for the scientist who attempts to study the human mind resembles a burglar attempting to open the vault of one of the world's major banks with a toothpick.

What are the consequences of the malleability of memory? One way to answer this question is to assume hypothetically that people have the potential for total mind malleability. Imagine a world in which people could go to a special kind of psychologist or psychiatrist — a memory doctor — and have their memories modified. Imagine clinics that specialize in memory modification treatment. One might go there once a week or once a month to have some particularly difficult memory altered. What therapeutic uses would this treatment have? How would our perceptions of the world change?

One could be treated for depression or feelings of worthlessness; the memory doctor would simply modify the memories leading to these feelings. One could have treatments to eliminate social prejudices; to the extent that these are based on a few incidents involving a unique group of people, the memory doctor could wipe out or alter memory of these incidents. One might also have treatments to increase happiness. If people feel bad because they are worse off than they once were, the memory doctor could eliminate the basis for comparison. And for improving marital relations, the memory doctor could enhance pleasant memories of past events involving the spouse. These memory modification specialists would be omnipotent. They would hold the key to total mind control.

This idea may seem far fetched since we obviously cannot now modify on command. But memory can be modified partially. Every day, we do this to ourselves and others. Each of the above extremes has its own milder parallel today. Our memories of past events change in helpful ways, leading us to be happier than we might otherwise be. It also changes, however, in harmful ways, and can occasionally cause us serious trouble.

About thirty years ago, in his *1984*, George Orwell wrote these words:

The control of the past depends above all on the training of memory . . . [It is] necessary to remember that events happened in the desired manner. And if it is necessary to rearrange one's memories or to tamper with written records, then it is necessary to forget that one has done so. The trick of doing this can be learned like any other mental techniques . . .

1984 is a few years away.

Elizabeth Loftus
University of Washington

1
The Power
of Memory

My father died five years ago, after he had engaged unwill-
ingly in a several-year battle with melanoma — "the deadliest of
all the cancers," he called it. As a physician, he knew only too
well. Whenever I thought about him the first few years after
his death, I could not escape the unpleasant images of his
illness. I remembered him in a hospital wheelchair waiting for
X-rays; I remembered him leaving the breakfast table unable
to eat; I remembered him in bed straining to move. I seemed
to remember only the sadness of the last year of his life. I tried
not to, but it appeared beyond my control. I wondered
whether I was to go through life thinking about my father in
only this way.

Then, gradually, my thoughts of him began to include
some happier images. I saw him standing in the yard, holding
a scrawny cat. I saw him in the living room surrounded by
smiling family. I even thought about him holding me on his
lap when I was no older than four. As nice as it was to have
my unpleasant memories of my father replaced by happier

images, I couldn't help but feel that there was something very curious about these "memories." And then I discovered that I have photographs of all of them. Pictures of our family when I was four are featured prominently in some old scrapbooks. A photo of him holding the cat has been in my wallet for years. Was I remembering my father or only the photographs of him?

The human mind, holder of vast memories, is intricately constructed. As Cicero said in *De Oratore*, "Memory is the treasury and guardian of all things." Without memory, life would consist of momentary experiences that have little relation to each other. Without memory we could not communicate with one another — we would be incapable of remembering the thoughts we wished to express. Without memory, a person would not have the sense of continuity even to know who he or she was. Without a doubt, memory is central to being human.

Most people don't stop to think about the pervasiveness of human memory, or about the many and varied ways in which memory — or the lack of it — has altered people's lives. Memory is a powerful force, even if it isn't always accurate. And it isn't. But before we can explore the physiological and psychological bases for memory's inaccuracy, it is important to look at displays of memory's power, such as total recall, and displays of its lack of power, as in amnesia. We should also consider the human ability to suppress unwanted memories and to dredge up those that are supposedly hidden or irretrievable.

Perhaps the person with total recall is the most familiar to us. We all remember someone brighter than the rest of us in school, someone who simply had a "head for facts" and could score perfectly on test after test. That person, we were often told, had total recall, a photographic memory that stored any piece of information, no matter how small.

Michael Barone is an information junkie who has a photographic memory. He collects facts about America. In college, he memorized the boundaries of every congressional district in the United States. He knew the results of just about every presidential election that took place in this century. He could also rattle off the populations of most major cities, and he could do this for different years. "What was the population of St. Louis in 1960?" someone once quizzed him. His reply: "750,026." He claims to do it by instinct. While honeymooning in Africa, he and his wife traveled over two thousand miles on roads too bumpy to allow them to read. He entertained her instead with facts. One day she learned all the winners of the vice-presidency; the next day she received a complete list of the losers.

When asked how long he'd been able to remember such minutiae so completely, Michael answered: "I was always interested in political numbers. I don't know why. I think I started working on census data when I was about eight or nine. I remember getting this map of the 1940 decennial census and being fascinated." He went on to say, grinning, "I think it's a neurotic disorder."

How astonishing is this ability? In 1968, Alexander Luria studied the unusual memory of a Russian newspaper reporter whom Luria referred to as S, which was the first letter of his name. Luria studied this man carefully over a span of many years. In the course of the investigation, it became clear that S could remember an incredible amount of information on a variety of topics after a brief and seemingly effortless examination. He could remember long lists of digits dictated to him and long lists of objects shown to him; he could store this material for any length of time and recall it at will. To accomplish this fantastic feat, S relied heavily on mental imagery. To remember a long grocery list, for example, he would imagine himself walking from Pushkin Square down Gorky Street and visualize each item at some specific point along his imaginary walk. He might "see" the eggs by a streetlamp or the bacon lying in a patch of grass. Later, when he wanted to remember the items, he simply repeated his imaginary walk to take a look at the objects where he had placed them.

In the early 1930s, S was asked to remember a formula

that was complex but totally nonsensical:

$$N \cdot \sqrt{d^2 \times \frac{85}{vx}} \cdot \sqrt[3]{\frac{276^2 \cdot 86x}{n^2v \cdot \pi 264}} \, n^2b \; = \; sv \, \frac{1624}{32^2} \cdot r^2s$$

He studied it for seven minutes and then reported how he memorized it. A portion of his response is typical of the kinds of stories he made up to help him remember things:

> Neiman [N] came out and jabbed at the ground with his cane [.]. He looked up at a tall tree which resembled the square-root sign [√], and thought to himself: "No wonder the tree has withered and begun to expose its roots. After all, it was here when I built these two houses" [d²]. Once again he poked with his cane [.]. Then he said: "The houses are old, I'll have to get rid of them [×]; the sale will bring in far more money." He had originally invested 85,000 in them [85]. . . .

The complete story was four times as long, but it must have been very powerful. Fifteen years later, with no advance warning, S could recall the formula perfectly.

People who are extremely good at remembering a large amount of material, like S and Michael Barone, are fairly unusual, although psychologists have shown that with sufficient practice many individuals can approximate the same level of performance. But the perfect-memory coin has a dark side. S often wished he could lose his perfect memory. His heavy reliance on mental imagery caused him difficulty: Past images continually intruded into his consciousness and interfered with his recall of later images; he occasionally became confused and found remembering very stressful; he had trouble holding down jobs because whenever anyone said anything to him, he would conjure up a long chain of thoughts, which made it difficult for him to understand what was being said to him. To earn a living he eventually became a professional theatrical memory man.

In contrast to Michael Barone and the newspaperman S, twenty-four-year-old Steven Kubacki underwent an ordeal more terrifying than one could possibly imagine — a total loss of memory. What Steven last remembers before the unusual chain of events is walking on the ice on Lake Michigan one Saturday in February 1978. He had planned to go cross-country skiing. At the edge of the lake, he took off his skis and dropped his backpack; it was a splendid place for solitude and thought. Then he began to get cold and decided to turn back, but in minutes he realized he was lost. He felt more and more numb, and he was getting tired. He next remembers waking up in a field and realizing it was spring. As he looked himself over, he recognized neither the backpack lying beside him nor any of his clothing. He thought to himself, "What the hell's going on here?" Later he said it felt like "the Twilight Zone or science fiction where all of a sudden people are misplaced in a strange land."

Steven started hiking to the nearest town. A stranger told him he was in Pittsfield, Massachusetts. A newspaper said it was May 5, 1979 — over fourteen months had passed since he left to go skiing. He managed to find his way to an aunt's home and knocked on her door: "She saw me," he relates. "She turned her head away. Then, she looked back and screamed, 'Steven!'"

Relatives came from all over to share in the happiness of his return. They naturally wanted to know where he had been for over a year, but he could tell them nothing. His backpack contained running shoes, swimming goggles, even a pair of glasses, but nothing he had ever owned before. He, more than anyone, has continued to be disturbed about those missing months.

How does someone remember everything? And how can a person's entire memory be wiped out for over a year? Do the memories exist in our mind's recesses, awaiting the right cue? Is approaching death one of those cues? Why is it that so many people who have almost died and then revived say that in those crucial moments their whole life passed before them?

In his memoir, Jacques Sandulescu recalls the winter of 1945 when, barely sixteen, he was arrested by Russian soldiers on his way to school in Brasov, Romania. All who seemed capable of work were packed into cattle cars and sent eastward into the Ukraine. The coal mines where he worked were treacherous. One day, weakened by cold, hunger, and illness, a daydreaming Jacques failed to jump out of the mine during a cave-in. He was buried alive. He couldn't move, not even to wiggle a toe. As sweat ran down his face, he cried and screamed but only succeeded in filling his mouth with choking coal dust. Fear overwhelmed him. His memoir recounts this moment:

> My childhood really did parade past me. I remembered finding some wild strawberries in the forest miles away from home. I had brought them to my mother inside a large green leaf; I knew how she loved them. As I gave them to her, she looked at them, the first strawberries of the season, and then gazed at me a long time. That look in her eyes was the most beautiful and tender thing I had known in my life.[1]

This "life review" is a mental process brought about by the realization, in the face of impending death, that immortality is a myth. Some individuals, like Sandulescu, have been rescued at precisely this moment and have thus lived to tell us about the experience. Typically, life review occurs spontaneously and rather unselectively, occurring in young people as well as old. People claim to have recalled certain life events with remarkable clarity, saying something like "I felt as though it happened only yesterday." Emotions at this time range from mildly pleasant nostalgia to feverish discomfort.

That such life review experiences occur so often prompts one to question the extent to which deeply buried memories are true. Did the young Romanian prisoner really find wild strawberries and give them to his mother in a large green leaf? Did she look at him tenderly? Since the Romanian's mother died long ago, we may never know.

Another way memories can be recalled into consciousness is through hypnosis. Although we normally associate hypnosis with the psychoanalytic process, psychiatrists aren't the only ones to use this device. In recent years, as crime-solving methods have grown more sophisticated, hypnosis has been used to help uncover missing pieces of evidence. One of the most highly publicized cases of this sort stunned the country in July of 1976, when a busload of twenty-six children mysteriously disappeared from the small California farming town of Chowchilla. Three masked men brandishing pistols had kidnapped the driver and driven them to a gravel quarry about a hundred miles away. All were forced into an abandoned trailer truck buried deeply underground; eventually, after more than sixteen hours had passed, they dug themselves out and were rescued.

The FBI moved in quickly to begin their investigation. One clue was the van that had been used by the suspects, but the school bus driver was unable to recall anything specific about it. To help crack the case, the Bureau called on an authority in hypnosis, who successfully made the driver recall all but one digit of the license plate on the kidnappers' white van. This was all that was needed to allow the Bureau to track down suspects and solve the case.

A police psychologist who was interviewed about the case marveled at the startling and fascinating results that law enforcement officials have achieved with hypnosis. He explained that hypnosis is a state of "heightened suggestibility" that "enhances certain aspects of human functioning, including memory." He further argued that "everything that ever happened to us or we perceive is registered in the brain. . . . Theoretically [using hypnotism], we can go back as far as we exist."

These beliefs are not new. Sigmund Freud encountered them in Europe nearly one hundred years ago. In the mid-1880s, Freud went to Paris to study with a noted French professor of anatomy, Jean Charcot, an experience that marked a turning point in his life. There was widespread belief that hypnosis could be used to cure psychological problems by getting people to relive certain early unhappy experiences. When Freud returned to Vienna the following year, he worked a great deal with hypnosis, but found it didn't always work very well. He renounced hypnosis as a useless therapeutic tool and instead developed the technique of "free association." By merely encouraging people to think about past episodes in their lives, Freud found they could dig up long-forgotten but important memories from their childhood. By analyzing these crucial life experiences, people often gained insight into their psychological problems.

Partially because of Freud's rejection of it, hypnosis was for quite some time deemed unfit for study in scientific laboratories. It wasn't until the early 1930s that hypnosis was again taken seriously by American behavioral psychologists. Yet now, after nearly fifty years of intensive study, it isn't really certain whether this mysterious process can be used to dig up actual memories. Is it true that everything that happens to us is registered in the brain — that with a bit of help from hypnosis or free association techniques we can remember it all? How did Freud know that his troubled patients were remembering the truth? Did he ever consider that his patients' versions of events in their past might be twisted or merely fabricated? As we shall see in Chapter 3, new insights in the field of human memory leave no doubt that people can have "memories" for things that never happened. And yet there are still even more perplexing cases of people who remember something they should never have heard, people who recall conversations after they have been anesthetized during an operation. It is hypnosis, in fact, that has been notably used to examine whether it is possible for a patient, while in an unconscious, anesthetized state, to be conscious, in some sense, of his or her surroundings. Can the seemingly unconscious patient register information?

California anesthesiologist William Miofsky was accused of several criminal counts of lewd and lascivious conduct for allegedly committing sodomy on female patients during surgery at a Sacramento hospital. Many civil suits were filed against him as well by women who generally could not remember anything about the surgery but feared they had been victims. Miofsky denied the allegations.

Some of the female patients involved in the Miofsky case were hypnotized to "unlock" their unconscious memories of what occurred during surgery. One patient who initially remembered nothing after surgery claimed later, under hypnosis, that she remembered a penis entering her mouth. When pressed for details, she provided them. Interestingly, though, she couldn't remember the knife cutting through her stomach. In response to this incident, one physician interviewed by a reporter for the Sacramento *Union* said that there is evidence anesthetized patients can recall minute details after surgery. This physician, seventy-six-year-old Dr. Milton H. Erickson, who seems to have devoted much of his life to hypnosis research, said that some patients can later remember entire conversations and physical actions of operating room personnel, even though they were in a deep state of unconsciousness.

Other examples also suggest that anesthetized people can hear and remember much more than surgeons believed possible. In one case, a female patient who had liked her surgeon before the surgery refused to go back to him. Under hypnosis she recalled hearing him utter these words during the operation: "Well, that will take care of this old bag!" In another study, patients were played tape recorded messages, some of which contained music, and some of which contained suggestions for comfort, good appetite, and rapid healing. Those who received the suggestions for quick recovery needed less medication and went home from the hospital earlier than those who had heard music.

One of the more carefully controlled studies was actually carried out in an operating room.[2] The physician who conducted the study was prompted to do it by an unusual experience. One of his patients was a young woman who had been in an accident, sustaining numerous facial injuries that required plastic surgery. During her operation, the doctor planned to remove a small lump from the inner surface of her lower lip. When the anesthetist was satisfied that the patient was deeply asleep, the surgeon put his finger in the patient's mouth and felt the lump. He said, "Good gracious. It may not be a cyst at all, it may be cancer!" Fortunately, the lump turned out to be benign.

In the ward a day later, the patient remembered entering the operating room and getting the injection, but nothing more. She complained of feeling very depressed and weepy. Three weeks later she was still depressed; she had lost her appetite and couldn't sleep. The doctor decided to hypnotize her and regress her to the time of the operation. In a flood of tears, she remembered everything. She even recalled the opening remark "Good gracious." She quoted the surgeon's statement, changing only the word *cancer* to *malignant*. Her doctor was amazed. He tried to reassure her, and then went on to design a more controlled study to explore this unusual phenomenon.

The doctor's study involved ten new patients. Anesthesia was induced by a combination of drugs, while the patients' EEG brain waves were monitored. At a specified point in time, when each patient's brain wave pattern indicated deep anesthetization, the anesthetist said something like:

Just a moment. I don't like the patient's color. The lips are too blue, very blue. More oxygen please. . . . Good, everything is fine now.

Each patient had an operation in which these remarks were made. When they were interviewed a month later, they remembered nothing about the operation. At this point, each patient was hypnotized and told to reexperience the operation. Four of the ten were able to "repeat practically verbatim the traumatic words used by the anesthetist. A further four patients displayed a severe degree of anxiety while reliving the operation. At the crucial moment, they woke from hypnosis and refused to participate further. The remaining two patients, though seemingly capable of reliving the operation under hypnosis, denied hearing anything."[3]

This research and certain others on recovery of memory under anesthesia suggest that it may be possible for a patient to remember sounds and words that were spoken. It is an old clinical adage that the last of the senses to go, whether a person is in a coma or under anesthesia, is the sense of hearing. This seems to tie in with the fact that there are virtually no reports of patients remembering the way things felt, looked, or smelled during surgery and that patients also seem unable to remember when the knife first cut their skin. It is not inconceivable that patients might be able to recover their other sense memories, but there is as yet no proof that this is possible. It is also possible that the patients, instead of remembering an event that took place during surgery, may simply be constructing that event from other "hospital" memories (TV shows, movies). The "memory" is then mistaken for reality. The disagreement among experts in the field forces one to suspend judgment about this issue until further evidence is secured. What is clear, however, is that to be unconscious, through anesthesia or through other means, is to be in an unusual and potentially alarming state, about which we have much to learn.

The opening essay in Carl Sagan's new book, *Broca's Brain: Reflections on the Romance of Science,* is set in a Paris museum that houses a large collection of human brains. The collection was begun by the famous French neurologist Paul Broca, who has been called the father of brain surgery. When Sagan stumbled across a bottle labeled "P. Broca," a sequence of thoughts was set off in his mind. Is it possible that in some mysterious sense Paul Broca is still in that container? Is it conceivable that scientists will someday be able to take one of these preserved brains, scan it, and extract its entire set of memories? (The ultimate breach in privacy!) Implicit in this notion is the belief that all of our memories are there to be potentially uncovered. As we shall see, this belief — widespread as it is — is currently undergoing a serious reexamination.

2
How Memory Works

The importance of memory is obvious. Without our ability to remember, we would live on the thin edge of today, unable to look back at yesterday. Memory gives life a certain richness — the pleasure of happy remembrances as well as the sorrow of unhappy ones. But memory is also a scientific mystery about which researchers have gradually discovered a number of clues.

When people think about memory, they usually think of it as a receptacle for facts. But memory is more complicated than just a mental warehouse stuffed with one's personal collection of experiences. It is a complex construct of experiences stored with particular attention to importance and accessibility. There are different ways to store information depending upon the length of time we want it remembered. Our memories separate input according to our need for it. If I meet a Ms. Meyer at a party and decide that it is important to remember her name, I might use the strategy of repeating her name out loud to myself, making sure it is firmly anchored in my consciousness. However, if I want to phone a restaurant to make a dinner reservation, I need only store the number long enough to make the call. Once the reservation is made, I no longer need to remember the number.

The processes of storing and receiving information are constantly interacting with one another. If strangers stop me on the street to ask, "Where is the nearest gas station?" I must store this question in memory long enough to understand it, search my memory for an answer, and then respond. They will then store my answer for as long as it is useful to them. Even the simplest conversation makes use of a set of rather complicated operations.

Every event and new piece of information does not immediately etch itself indelibly into our memories. Rather, there are at least three distinct stages to a memory system, and information must pass through all of them in order to be remembered for more than a half minute or so. The system's three memory stages are called sensory register, short-term memory (STM), and long-term memory (LTM).

Suppose you are browsing through a bookstore and notice a book. After a quick glance, you might notice the book's title, and you might even remember the color of its jacket. But the actual process of storing and remembering this information is more complex. First, the information on the cover enters your memory system by means of a sense organ, in this case the eyes. That experience dictates a purely sensory memory, which briefly holds a virtually literal record of the image. That image will decay quickly, however, disappearing in less than a second or so. If the information is to last longer, it must be transferred quickly to short-term memory.

Short-term memory is an active memory, sometimes equated with consciousness since it holds the contents of your attention. If you think constantly about a fact, you can keep it indefinitely in STM. You use STM to hold information when, for example, you look up a telephone number and repeat it to yourself while going to dial it. What we choose to keep in STM is largely a matter of personal interest. Whereas

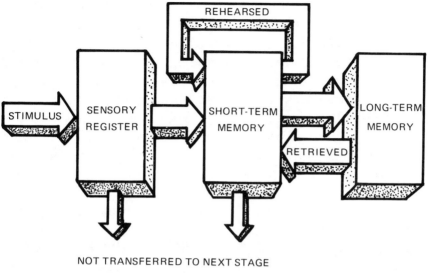

REHEARSED

STIMULUS

SENSORY REGISTER

SHORT-TERM MEMORY

LONG-TERM MEMORY

RETRIEVED

NOT TRANSFERRED TO NEXT STAGE
AND THEREFORE FORGOTTEN

The memory process: Incoming information enters short-term memory, where it can be maintained by rehearsal and successfully transferred to long-term memory, or forgotten.

one person might look at a billboard and remember that the advertisement is for a new style of car, another might recall the fact that the new model is on sale. Unless you consciously attend to information in STM, it will decay within fifteen to twenty seconds.

Long-term memory is the largest component of the memory system. It is practically limitless, resembling a huge library with millions of books stashed away on the shelves. Every so often we add hundreds of new books to the library, and it seems as if we never run out of shelf space. It has been estimated that in a lifetime, long-term memory records as many as one quadrillion separate bits of information.[1] Long-term memory holds information only a few minutes old, such as points made earlier in a conversation. It also stores information several decades old, such as an older person's reminiscences of childhood.

How does all this information get into long-term memory? It begins with a brief stay in STM; if it is mulled over there for a while, it enters LTM. The longer we think about a new fact, the longer it stays in STM and the greater its chances of moving into LTM. Put another way, if we rehearse new information, it is transferred from STM to LTM. This happens when we deliberately try to memorize, as well as when we simply think about material just encountered. If we rehearsed or thought about the fact that a billboard advertised the sale price of a new car model, we would likely store this information in our long-term memories.

Suppose we are asked a simple question such as what the sale price is. With the millions of pieces of information stored in memory, how do we find the answer to this question quickly? Current opinion is that we check STM for the information; if we are unable to find an answer, we begin searching LTM. Upon its recall, information is temporarily transferred back to STM, where we can consciously think about it. From STM, we can produce the information out loud, responding to the original question.

Let's look at this whole process a little more closely.

Sensory Memory

Under normal conditions, your eye holds on to an image for only a fraction of a second before the image is replaced by another. If you are walking along a busy street and approach a red traffic signal, the image of the signal first reaches your eye. It is then processed by the visual system, and eventually by the brain. Memory begins when the image of the traffic signal enters the sensory register, or sensory memory. Sensory memory holds this image in rich detail, as would a photograph. But the contents of this memory constantly change as new stimuli arrive. The image lasts here very briefly, and unless it enters short-term or long-term memory, it is lost. Thus, sensory memory is a sort of photographic memory.

In point of fact, we don't have just one sensory memory, we have several. One holds information that we pick up with our eyes; another holds information from our ears, and so on for all of our sensory modalities. If, as you are walking along that same busy street, a car backfires behind you, the sound reaches your ear and enters an auditory sensory memory. The sensory image is held in a fairly complete form, but only briefly.

Interestingly, the sensory image from a sound disappears somewhat more slowly than the sensory image from a sight. When you turn off a radio, a trace of the sound seems to linger. Something similar happens when you flash a picture very briefly in front of your eyes: A trace of the image persists momentarily, but not quite as long. In the typical procedure for testing the length of these traces, first invented by George Sperling, subjects shown a group of letters at lightning-fast speed had to recall as many as they could. On the average, only four or five letters could be recalled, whether the subjects had been shown six, nine, or more. But if one of several audible tones was sounded just after the letters were removed, indicating which single row of letters to report, the subjects could recall the correct row with practically no mistakes. Since the subjects had no idea which row from the entire display would have to be recalled, they must have had all the letters of the display in their memory immediately after the letters were removed. At the tone, the chosen letters were isolated and recalled; in the process, the rest of the letters were allowed to fade. The photographic image is brief, lasting only a fraction of a second. The image in sensory memory fades quickly, and we then rely on that which has been transferred into more permanent memory.

Short-term Memory

If we focus attention on any information from our environment, such as the red traffic signal, it may enter short-term memory. However, when we focus on one thing, we take attention away from others. If we are doing something that we have learned very well, there is no problem, and we can devote more attention to other activities at the same time. Most people can drive a car and carry on a conversation, and perhaps even eat an apple, all at the same time. If things are made difficult, as in the case of a blizzard, driving the car may require our complete attention, and simultaneous apple-munching may be impossible. Did you ever notice that when you're having trouble following traffic directions or need to watch for a specific street sign, your first instinct is to turn the radio off or shush your passengers?

When a person stands in the midst of others at a crowded cocktail party carrying on a conversation, it is usually easy to concentrate on that conversation. If the person hears his or her own name from a different conversation, attention may be diverted momentarily. This is a good example of what William James meant when he said that attention "implies withdrawal from some things in order to deal effectively with others." We withdraw from the conversation in which we are engaged so that we can attend to the one in which our name has been mentioned. The "cocktail party phenomenon," as it has been called, shows that people can shift attention almost instantaneously. It also shows that we attend to what interests us, what is pertinent to us, and what is meaningful for us.

Most importantly, however, attention determines what gets into short-term memory. Since we are selective about the focus of attention, much of what we are exposed to will never even enter this next memory stage and be available for later retrieval. Many of the problems that we think of as memory difficulties are probably due to lapses of attention. If we had just pulled out of a gas station and someone asked what kind of shoes the station attendant was wearing, we would not be able to answer if we hadn't noticed the shoes in the first place.

Short-term memory cannot hold very much. An incident that happened to my neighbor, Mrs. Thompson, shows the limited capacity of STM. One day she developed a splitting headache and went home to lie down. Her head had hardly touched the pillow when the phone rang. A voice at the other end said, "Mrs. Thompson, this is the Sheraton Hotel in Chicago calling. Your husband's plane has been delayed in Chicago and he had to change to a new plane. Instead of the old flight number 141, his new flight number is 98. And instead of getting in at 8:22, he won't be in until 11:13. He asked that you pick him up at the gate instead of at the baggage area. I must go now; I have several other calls to make. Goodbye." Mrs. Thompson, with headache pounding, had no more than put the receiver down and turned to look for a pencil when she realized that all the information was gone. Typically, STM cannot hold on to more than six or seven items at one time. The moment information enters STM, it seems clear and is quite easy to recall if done so immediately. The classic example of short-term memory, mentioned earlier, is the recall of an unfamiliar telephone number. If you look up a number in your phone book, you can repeat it to someone else or dial it yourself. In a moment or so, you will probably not be able to remember it. Of course you can repeat the phone number to yourself or aloud, a process called rehearsal, and this will prevent its rapid decay from STM.

Ordinarily, without rehearsal, short-term memory cannot retain anything for more than a half minute or so. This fact is shown in a study in which subjects were given several letters to remember. Then they were given a difficult arithmetic task to keep them from repeating the letters to themselves.[2] After only eighteen seconds, subjects could recall very little of what they had been shown.

It is probably to our advantage that information is forgotten quickly. There are many times in life when we have no need to remember information very long. If we did, it would only get in our way. A store clerk, for example, might remember only briefly that customer A handed over a ten-dollar bill and needs $1.25 in change. By the time customer B comes along, the amount of change given to A has vanished from memory. It is as if we deliberately forget.

One reason short-term memory is so important is that it plays a crucial role in conscious thought. When we think about who was at a recent party or what we need to buy at the grocery store, we are using our short-term memories. We also need short-term memory to provide the gateway through which information may pass into long-term memory.

Long-term Memory

If we are ever to avoid repeating mistakes and gain from our past experiences, then information from our environment must find its way into long-term memory. The process, sometimes called "transfer," seems to take place in a straightforward way. New information held in short-term memory can be kept alive if repeated or rehearsed. It is then associated with any relevant pieces of information that may already exist in long-term memory. The new information is then added to what already exists.

Human beings who have undergone electric shock therapy are a source of information about the workings of memory. In this therapy, severe electric shocks are delivered to the brain, often to patients suffering from severe depression. One major side effect of this treatment is some memory loss. Typically, the patients forget what they learned immediately before the shock. The shock seems to erase the memory so fully that little can be detected later on. If the shocks are delayed so that the information has had a chance to get into long-term memory, the recollection is much less likely to be disrupted. Experiments with animals have shown the same results. A rat who had just learned a new trick followed by the application of electroconvulsive shock (ECS) cannot remember the trick anymore. It is as if the shock "shook up" the information and prevented it from getting into LTM.[3]

The effect of electrical shock on memory is a bit more complicated than I've stated it so far. There are cases in which a memory lost immediately after shock treatment is recovered later. For example, just before treatment, a patient met a new member of the hospital staff, Dr. McCarthy; afterward, he could not recall the name. With a few hints ("the name starts with the letter *M*"), the name popped up. This means that some of the information may have crept into long-term memory — not enough for unprompted recall, but enough so that clues helped. It is likely that shock treatment interferes with the transfer from STM to LTM, although it does not prevent it completely.

A specific structure in the brain, called the hippocampus, seems to play a major role in the transfer of information from short- to long-term memory. We know this from detailed analyses of patients who have had part of their hippocampus removed. Take the case of patient H. M., who had part of his brain removed to treat severe epilepsy. The treatment succeeded in curing the epilepsy but caused H. M. to develop a profound memory defect. His short-term memory was quite normal and his long-term recall of information acquired before the operation remained intact. But he could no longer get new information into his long-term memory. It is easy to appreciate what life might be like if we could not form new memories by reading a neuropsychologist's description of H. M.'s behavior and feelings:

> This young man (H. M.) . . . had had no obvious memory disturbance before his operation, having, for example, passed his high school examinations without difficulty. (He sustained) a minor head injury at the age of 7. Minor (seizures) began one year later, and then, at the age of 16, he began to have generalized seizures which, despite heavy medication, increased in frequency and severity until, by the age of 27, he was no longer able to work . . . ; his prospects were by then so desperate that the radical bilateral medial temporal lobe (surgery) . . . was performed. The patient was drowsy for the first few postoperative days but then, as he became more alert, a severe memory impairment was apparent.

He could no longer recognize the hospital staff, apart from (the surgeon), whom he had known for many years; he did not remember and could not relearn the way to the bathroom, and he seemed to retain nothing of the day-to-day happenings in the hospital. His early memories were seemingly vivid and intact, his speech was normal, and his social behavior and emotional responses were entirely appropriate.

There has been little change in this clinical picture during the years which have elapsed since the operation . . . there (is no) evidence of general intellectual loss; in fact, his intelligence as measured by standard tests is actually a little higher now than before the operation. . . . Yet the remarkable memory defect persists, and it is clear that H. M. can remember little of the experiences of the last . . . years. . . .

Ten months after the operation, the family moved to a new house which was situated only a few blocks away from their old one, on the same street. When examined . . . nearly a year later, H. M. had not yet learned the new address, nor could he be trusted to find his way home alone, because he would go to the old house. Six years ago, the family moved again, and H. M. is still unsure of his present address, although he does seem to know that he has moved. (The patient) . . . will do the same jigsaw puzzles day after day without showing any practice effect, and read the same magazines over and over again without finding their contents familiar. . . .

Even such profound amnesias as these are, however, compatible with a normal attention span. . . . On one occasion, he was asked to remember the number 584 and was then allowed to sit quietly with no interruption for 15 minutes, at which point he was able to recall the number correctly without hesitation. When asked how he had been able to do this, he replied,

"It's easy. You just remember 8. You see 5, 8, and 4 add to 17. You remember 8; subtract it from 17 and it leaves 9. Divide 9 in half and you get 5 and 4, and there you are: 584. Easy."

In spite of H. M.'s elaborate mnemonic scheme he was unable, a minute or so later, to remember either the number 584 or any of the associated complex train of thought; in fact, he did not know that he had been given a number to remember. . . .

One gets some idea of what such an amnesic state must be like from H. M.'s own comments. . . . Between tests, he would suddenly look up and say, rather anxiously,

"Right now, I'm wondering. Have I done or said anything amiss? You see, at this moment everything looks clear to me, but what happened just before? That's what worries me. It's like waking from a dream. I just don't remember."[4]

H. M.'s syndrome is fascinating in terms of what he can and cannot remember. In general, he can register new information quite normally in short-term memory, but it quickly becomes unavailable to him. Also significant is that this problem does not seem to occur when he learns a new motor skill such as playing tennis. Remarkably, he seems to have normal long-term memory for newly learned motor skills, even though he has no long-term memory for most other kinds of information. This observation seems to indicate that motor skill learning and memory are very different from other kinds of learning and memory. We have always known that motor skill learning is very resistant to loss — for example, you never *do* really forget how to ride a bicycle! Observations of H. M. seem to indicate that motor skill memory may be different in other ways as well.

Imagine this scenario. Two roommates, Mary and Jane, are planning a party. Mary is to do all the shopping while Jane has agreed to do the cooking. On her way home from work, Mary stops at the market and realizes that she has forgotten to bring the grocery list. She calls Jane and asks her to read the grocery list. Rather than write it down, Mary insists she'll remember it if Jane recites it to her. "Eggs, butter, cookies, hamburger, catsup, pepper, onions, milk, cheese, bread, peanuts, and pickles," Jane itemizes to Mary.

A moment after hanging up the phone, Mary finds a pencil and writes down the items that Jane read to her, just as she remembers them. When the shopping is finished, Mary carts her bag of groceries home and hands it over to Jane. When the bag is emptied, Jane turns, somewhat annoyed, and says, "How can I possibly make dinner! You forgot the catsup, pepper, onions, and milk!"

Does Mary have a rotten memory? Perhaps not. In fact, she has illustrated a classic example: When people are given a list of items to remember, the items at the beginning and at the end of the list are remembered well, while items from the middle of the list are remembered more poorly. The fact that the first few items have a good chance of being remembered has been called the "primacy effect." The fact that the last few items have a good chance of being remembered has been called the "recency effect." If one hundred people were given Mary and Jane's shopping list to remember, and we graphed the number who remembered each item, we would see the classic "serial position curve" shown opposite.

We explain the serial position curve because of the operation of both STM and LTM. Mary remembered peanuts and pickles, the items at the end of the list, because they were in short-term memory at the moment when she found her pencil and began to try to remember the list. They were likely to be in short-term memory because no later items displaced them. After Mary had "dumped out" the contents of her short-term memory, she then began searching long-term memory. She remembered eggs and butter, items at the beginning of the

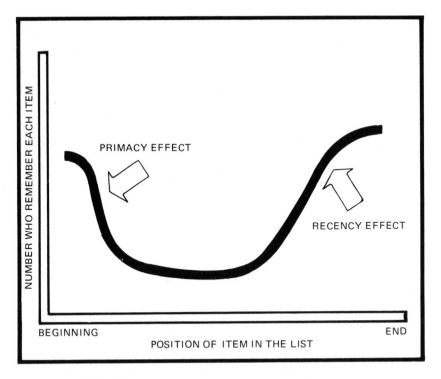

The serial position curve

list, because these items had been transferred into long-term memory. Items at the beginning of the list have the best chance of getting into LTM because they get more attention than other items. At the moment that Jane mentioned the first item, eggs, Mary devoted her full attention to that item. When the next one, butter, came along, she turned her attention to this, but also tried to "hang on" to the first item. When Jane read the third item, Mary heard it, but was also trying to concentrate on the first two items. Studies in which people have been presented with a list of words to remember have confirmed this explanation. If people are asked to say aloud whatever word they are thinking as the list is being presented to them, it is easy to see that the first word momentarily gets full attention, while later words share attention.

"I remember opening the can, and I remember washing the pot, but I don't remember eating the chili."

(*Drawing by Frascino;* © 1979 The New Yorker *Magazine, Inc.*)

An item in the middle of the list will be remembered well if unusual in some way. If one of the items on the grocery list had been a copy of *Playgirl* magazine, Mary might have remembered it no matter where in the list it occurred. The fact that an odd item is typically easy to remember has been called the "Von Restorff effect," after the psychologist who first discovered it.

The Giant Warehouse of Our Mind

When we think about memory, we are usually thinking of long-term memory. Some psychologists have likened STM and LTM to a desk. The top of the desk is like STM while the drawers or files are like LTM. Letters, papers, and other materials on top of it are gathered from diverse sources, both from current incoming inputs and from the files of information stored in LTM. The materials assembled on the top of the desk may be used to answer a letter or to solve a particular problem. When they are not needed any longer, they may be filed away in a drawer or filing cabinet. Memory is tidy: Material that is taken from one of the files can be returned to its place after it has been used. But this analogy is not perfect; material temporarily placed in STM is not really removed from LTM.

Long-term memory is more or less thought of as a permanent storehouse of facts. It contains all the events of a lifetime. It is practically limitless, and there seems to be no risk of overloading long-term memory, which is remarkable given the relatively small space in our brains. But storage is not the problem. In order for this vast library of knowledge to be useful to us, there must be some plan or scheme to the way the information is arranged. Otherwise, we would not be able to find anything. Somewhere in each person's brain lives a superb librarian.

How is long-term memory arranged? The analogy to a library and its card catalog, or to a book and its index, seems to be a useful one. The card catalog or book index is used as a way of finding any material that we need. Similarly, we use "indexes" to call up information that is cataloged in long-term memory. We might get to our memory of Aunt Beth's swimming pool by thinking of swimming pools in general or hearing the words our sister remarked, "Remember last summer at Aunt Beth's. . . ." The more ways we have to index a piece of information or the more associations we have with it, the easier it is to remember. It is important to keep in mind that we don't file away film clips or tape recordings of our experience. Rather, we store bits and pieces of our experience. A particularly happy birthday party may have lasted three hours, but if a friend took that long to tell you about it, you might find him quite dull indeed. The brain condenses experiences for us. It seems to edit the boring parts in order to highlight the interesting parts and cross-reference them for storage. While there are many similarities in the ways in which different people's memories are organized, each memory is also unique. This is because memory is a result of a collection of life experiences, and everybody's life experiences are different.

A study of "mental maps" — conceptual pictures we make of our environment — shows how our worlds map into memory differently. Three groups of people living in the Los Angeles area were asked to draw a mental map of L.A.; their drawings were affected by where they lived and by what social class they came from.[5] The mental maps of upper-middle-class whites from Westwood were vastly more detailed than the maps produced by either black residents living near Watts or Spanish-speaking people in the Boyle Heights area. The upper-middle-class people pictured their city as a sprawling one with lots of interesting areas surrounding their specific neighborhood. Their mental pictures spanned great distances, from the Pacific Ocean north to the San Fernando Valley, east beyond the downtown area and as far south as Long Beach. The version produced by the black residents in Avalon near Watts, however, was a much more restricted map that included little more than the main streets leading to the city center. Outlying areas such as Santa Monica were not connected securely to the immediate area in which they lived. Finally, maps from the Hispanic group pictured little more than a few streets, City Hall, and the bus depot, obviously the major means by which a majority of these people leave and return to their small world. Clearly, many complex factors enter into a person's mental image of his or her environment. Each person's mental map is riddled with unique spatial biases. Each person's memory, however, is rich in its own way.

Another illustration of the unique spatial bias of memory can be seen in "The Bostonian's Idea of the United States." Daniel Wallingford's humorous map cuts at the sharp edge of truth. To Bostonians, their city is at the hub of New England. New England is seen as the major region of the country and

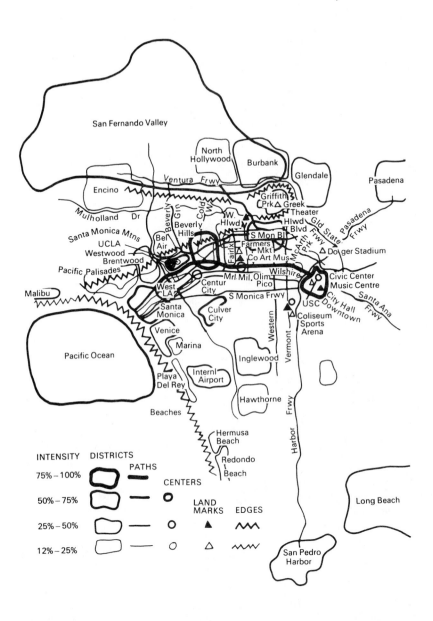

Mental maps: On this page we see Los Angeles through the eyes of upper-middle-class white persons in Westwood; on the following page are quite different representations by both black and Spanish-speaking residents (Gould and White, 1974).

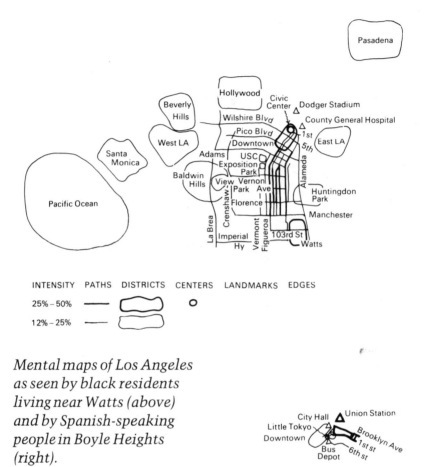

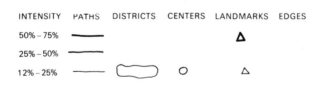

*Mental maps of Los Angeles
as seen by black residents
living near Watts (above)
and by Spanish-speaking
people in Boyle Heights
(right).*

thus assumes gigantic proportions in the Bostonian mind. Cape Cod is a monumental stretch of land, reaching out for commerce and culture from the rest of the earth. New York City and Washington, D.C., being somewhat brash new towns, are relegated to their appropriate places in the hinterland. Obviously, they are merely stopping points on one's way

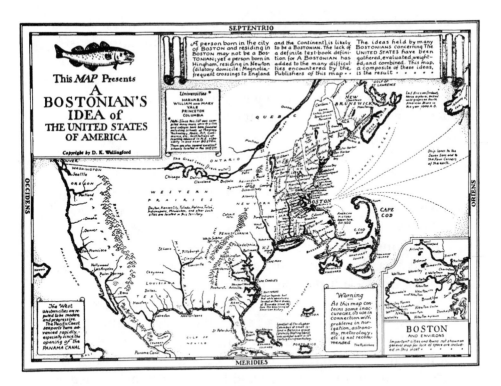

*The Bostonian's view of the United States
(Gould and White, 1974)*

to the western prairies. Pittsburgh is somewhat near St. Louis, and most of the Midwest simply is lumped together.

Rummaging Through Mental Drawers

Retrieving information from long-term memory is another remarkable ability that most of us take for granted. The retrieval schemes we possess are crucial for an efficient memory. Reconsidering the library analogy, suppose you had a collection of books, none of which had indexes. You decide you want to read something about drugs. Without an index, you might have to skim through entire books, page by page, before you came across some information on drugs. That could take days or even weeks. But by using an index, you can find out in minutes where some useful information exists.

Long-term memory is similarly accessible through an indexlike apparatus. This is what allows us to retrieve what we need in a matter of seconds or less. Ask someone for the name of his children, or his telephone number, or who the President of the United States is, and typically, giving the answer is effortless. This means that we must have fairly direct access to a lot of information stored in LTM.

When we try to remember something from our past, we often rely on *cues.* Cues help us check different parts of long-term memory to see if any of them contain the fact we are looking for. If you want to remember a parakeet you owned as a child, you may begin thinking about little birds. Your brain doesn't pull out mental images of horses or cows or roller coasters — presumably because these are stored elsewhere. If you once owned a pet parakeet named Jimmy (as I did), you could retrieve memories of Jimmy by first thinking of his name. (Thinking of Jimmy leads me to remember the time when Jimmy flew away and I — at age eight — cried all night until a neighbor, who found him huddling in a tree hole, brought him back the next day.) If you couldn't remember what kind of pet you had at all, you might begin thinking about the kinds of pets that people usually have — dogs, cats, canaries, hamsters, turtles. Eventually when cued with "parakeet," you very well might remember Jimmy. This is the power of cues.

Almost anything can serve as a retrieval cue. A sight. A smell. A word. Flames pouring from a burning pot on the stove can bring to mind all we know about fires. On the other hand, gas leaking from the stove, particularly if it is odorless and colorless, cannot serve as a retrieval cue. Smoke as a cue is a little better, but it is often subtle, especially if we are asleep; thus, it cannot serve as a really good cue. A smoke detector's piercing sound is a mechanical cue to warn us of danger.

In a legal court, the notion of retrieval cues is important, although they are not usually called by that name. Witnesses who cannot remember important details are asked a question or handed a memorandum to spur their recollection. In theory, anything that actually refreshes a witness's memory may be used. Some courts have waxed poetic, declaring that the refresher could be "a song, or a face, or a newspaper item" (*Jewitt* v. *United States*, 1926), or "the creaking of a hinge, the whistling of a tune, the smell of seaweed, the sight of an old photograph, the taste of nutmeg, the touch of a piece of canvas" (*Fanelli* v. *U.S. Gypsum Co.*, 1944).

In the literary world, there is a fascination with anything that succeeds in recalling the past. Marcel Proust put it most beautifully in *Swann's Way:*

> . . . the smell and taste of things remain poised a long time, like souls, ready to remind us, waiting and hoping for their moment, amid the ruins of all the rest; and bear unfaltering, in the tiny and almost impalpable drop of their essence, the vast structure of recollection.

> And once I had recognized the taste of the crumb of Madeleine soaked in her decoction of lime flowers, which my aunt used to give me (although I did not yet know and must long postpone the discovery of why this memory made me so happy) immediately the old grey house upon the street, where her room was, rose up like the scenery of a theatre to attach itself to the little pavilion, opening on to the garden, . . . ; and with the house the town, from morning to night and in all weathers, the Square where I was sent before luncheon, the streets along which I used to run errands, the country roads we took when it was fine.

3
How Memory Doesn't Work

In Anatole France's book *Penguin Island*, the chapter called "The Dragon of Alca" is immensely interesting. It is about a frightful dragon who supposedly had ravaged the Penguin people, a peaceful group who ordinarily inhabited Alca in tranquillity. One day a beautiful maiden, Orberosia, disappeared. At first, her absence caused no uneasiness because she had often been carried off by men who were consumed by their love for her. But when she did not return, the Penguin people feared that the dragon had devoured her. Later, a young orphan and several animals also disappeared, providing proof of the existence of the dragon. The village elders finally assembled to figure out what to do about the terrible circumstances. They called together all Penguins who had seen the dragon during the disastrous night and asked them:

"Have you noticed his form and his behavior?"

And each answered in his turn:

"He has the claws of a lion, the wings of an eagle, and the tail of a serpent."

"His back bristles with thorny crests."

"His whole body is covered with yellow scales."

"His look fascinates and confounds. He vomits flames."

"He poisons the air with his breath."

"He has the head of a dragon, the claws of a lion, and the tail of a fish."

And a woman of Anis, who was regarded as intelligent and of sound judgment and from whom the dragon had taken three hens, deposed as follows:

"He is formed like a man. The proof is that I thought he was my husband, and I said to him, 'Come to bed, you old fool.'"

Others said:

"He is formed like a cloud."

"He looks like a mountain."

And a child came and said:

"I saw the dragon taking off his head in the barn so that he might give a kiss to my sister Minnie."

And the Elders also asked the inhabitants:

"How big is the dragon?"

And it was answered:

"As big as an ox."

"Like the big merchant ships of the Bretons."

"He is the height of a man."

"He is higher than the fig-tree under which you are sitting."

"He is as large as a dog."

Questioned finally on his color, the inhabitants said:

"Red."

"Green."

"Blue."

"Yellow."

"His head is bright green, his wings are brilliant orange tinged with pink, his limbs are silver grey, his hind-quarters and his tail are striped with brown and pink bands, his belly bright yellow spotted with black."

"His colour? He has no colour."

"He is the colour of a dragon."

In this passage Anatole France said much about his view of memory; namely, that people differ in what they think they remember. Each individual is unique. Each is the product of his or her inheritance and environment. Each has a unique memory. Even identical twins who have lived in what seems like identical environments have different experiences and thus different memories.

Memory is imperfect. This is because we often do not see things accurately in the first place. But even if we take in a reasonably accurate picture of some experience, it does not necessarily stay perfectly intact in memory. Another force is at work. The memory traces can actually undergo distortion. With the passage of time, with proper motivation, with the introduction of special kinds of interfering facts, the memory traces seem sometimes to change or become transformed. These distortions can be quite frightening, for they can cause us to have memories of things that never happened. Even in the most intelligent among us is memory thus malleable.

The Malleability of Memory

Three myths about Sigmund Freud's life are widely accepted: that he lived all his life at the cutting edge of poverty; that he suffered continually because of discrimination against Jews, including being denied university appointments; and that he was ignored and neglected by Viennese physicians and others in his intellectual community.

Whether these myths are true or distortions has been the subject of great debate. Some deny the myths, alleging instead that Freud made good money as a doctor, that he was not discriminated against until very late in life when Hitler drove him into exile, and that he achieved enormous recognition and academic honors.

What is most interesting about these myths is that Freud himself believed them. Not only did he invent them, he publicized them. Throughout his letters, he stressed them; obviously they were important to him. Why? One explanation that has been advanced is a Freudian one: The myths are Freudian slips.[1]

According to Peter Drucker, who knew Freud's family, Freud suffered from "poorhouse neurosis," the secret and suppressed obsession with money. The poorhouse neurosis shows itself in a continual fear of ending up poor and a constant nagging worry about not having enough. His own neurosis has been used to explain why he could not notice that his parents were actually comfortably middle class and that he himself was living quite a comfortable life. This was simply repressed.

As to the complaints that he was the victim of anti-Semitism, these too covered up another fact; namely, his inability to tolerate non-Jews. He could not admit, especially to himself, that he found the non-Jew "irksome, difficult, a stranger, and an irritation." He dealt with this conflict by coming to believe that it was they who were rejecting him.

And finally, he complained that he was ignored by Viennese physicians. In fact, they discussed him, doubted him, and rejected him but did not ignore him. But this was too painful for Freud to accept, so he covered up his belief by suggesting that they were ignoring him.

Others in Freud's time managed to distort their memories similarly. Many doctors in the Nazi hierarchy have been studied by Yale psychiatrist Robert Jay Lifton, who asked himself how these doctors could possibly continue to regard themselves so favorably, given what they had done. Could they possibly have forgotten the terrible things they perpetrated? Lifton has concluded that they use a very effective form of self-delusion called "middle knowledge." Middle knowledge is a form of knowing and not knowing at the very same time. One doctor involved in shipping large amounts of cyanide to the Nazi death camps was genuinely shocked when told the cyanide had been used to exterminate people. Lifton commented: "He had worked very hard not to know."[2]

This brings to mind the term *Pentimento*, the title of a book by Lillian Hellman and a way of referring to a painter who paints over a painting, as if he had *repented* or changed his mind. Even so, part of the original painting, like memories, may show vaguely through the overlay.

The alleged distortions in portions of Freud's memory may seem unusual, but they are not. The same sorts of distortions occur when people's memories are tested in a controlled laboratory situation. A classic example is the case where subjects were shown an illustration of several people on a subway car, including a black man with a hat and a white man with a razor in his hand. Using the method of serial reproduction where one person describes the picture to another, who describes it to another — much like the childhood game of "telephone" — two investigators found that the razor tended to migrate in memory from the white man to the black man. One person reported, "This is a subway train in New York headed for Portland Street. There is a Jewish woman and a Negro who has a razor in his hand. The woman has a baby or a dog. The train is going to Dyer Street and nothing much happened."[3] How does someone create so detailed an image? And why do people remember the razor in the hands of the black man? In this case, stereotypes are affecting what they see and remember.

When we try to remember something that happened to us, these sorts of "constructive" errors are common. We can usually recall a few facts, and using these facts we construct other facts that probably happened. We make inferences. From these probable inferences, we are led to other "false facts" that might — or might not — have been true. To paraphrase C. S. Morgan, we fill up the lowlands of our memories from the highlands of our imaginations. This process of using inferences and probable facts to fill in the gaps of our memories has been called "refabrication," and it probably occurs in nearly all of our everyday perceptions. We supply these bits and pieces, largely unconsciously, to round out fairly incomplete knowledge.

We fill in gaps in our memory using chains of events that are logically acceptable. There are so many real-life illustrations of this to choose from. For example, a taxi traveling on a busy street makes an emergency stop. A passenger in the taxi sees that a red Buick in front has stopped abruptly, its right-hand door is open, and an elderly man is lying unconscious on the street. The passenger assumes that the man either fell or was thrown out the door of the Buick and remembers seeing this happen. In fact, the driver of the Buick had stepped on his brakes suddenly so as to avoid hitting the older man who had wandered into the intersection. The collision was unavoidable and the man was knocked to the ground. The only thing the passenger actually saw was the unconscious man lying on the ground and the open door of the Buick. These fragments were then integrated into a logical sequence and a new "memory" was created. Our biases, expectations, and past knowledge are all used in the filling-in process, leading to distortions in what we remember.

These distortions force us to ask a fundamental question. Although it may seem as if a person has forgotten some important idea (like·Freud's "forgetting" his financial situation, or people "forgetting" that it was a white man who had the razor), have they truly forgotten it? Is there any way in which we could get a person to become aware of these "forgotten" facts? Are they there to be found? Or are they lost?

Do Memories Last Forever?

Few people would deny the existence of the very prevalent experience that we call "forgetting." This is the common occurrence of having facts, events, and details in our memory become less available as time passes. It is obvious that there are items we once knew that seem to be forgotten; they cannot be recalled. Yet a fundamental question remains to be answered: Does forgetting mean that the items are irretrievably lost? *Or* have they simply been overlaid with other material so that they cannot be found? The notion that they have been overlaid suggests that the door to memory could be unlocked, if one could only produce the key, and the crucial memory would then come tumbling out.

Freud, whose private medical practice predominantly attracted individuals suffering from a variety of "nervous disorders," is perhaps one of the best known individuals to put forth the view that memory is in some sense permanent. In treating his patients, Freud thought it necessary to trace his patients' symptoms — such as tremors, tics, and paralysis — back to more remote memories, to the early and seemingly conmon amnesia that covers early childhood up to about the age of five. In order to understand a particular hysterical symptom, Freud argued, one must reach back into the earliest years of childhood. He reasoned that these early experiences, typically forgotten, must have been crucial. By forgotten, Freud did not mean that these memories were lost forever. Rather, in his classic work, *Psychopathology of Everyday Life*, he claimed that

> . . . all impressions are preserved, not only in the same form in which they were first received, but also in all

the forms which they have adopted in their further developments. . . . Theoretically every earlier state of the mnemonic content could thus be restored to memory again, even if its elements have long ago exchanged all their original connections for more recent ones.[4]

Despite his preoccupation with nervous patients, Freud observed that everyone suffers failures of memory. Repressed traces of memory suffer no change, he argued, even over very long periods of time. A wise commentator on Freud reminds us of a clinical anecdote from the early nineteenth century: An illiterate young woman had a seizure of "nervous fever" during which she could recite at length in Latin, Greek, and Hebrew. Her physicians were puzzled until they discovered that many years before, the young woman had been a servant in the household of an elderly Protestant pastor. It had been the custom of this pastor to pace up and down a hallway next to the kitchen reading aloud to himself from one of his favorite books. Apparently the young woman had absorbed these sounds, even though for her they had no meaning, and under the stress of her mental illness they had emerged from the recesses of her mind. This anecdote gave support to the thesis that "all thoughts are in themselves imperishable."[5] Freud held that our impressions — even those from infancy — have never really been lost but are "only inaccessible and latent, having become part of the unconscious."[6]

Is there anything to this idea that all thoughts are imperishable, that no impressions are ever really forgotten? Is it common for people to believe in this idea, or were Freud's ideas unusual?

Not too long ago I conducted an informal survey to find out what people believe about the permanence of memory.[7] I asked 169 individuals from various parts of the United States to give their views about how memory works. These people had varied occupations; while some of them had had some formal training in the field of psychology, most had not. Some were lawyers, some were secretaries, some were taxicab drivers; others were physicians or philosophers. There were a few fire investigators, and even an eleven-year-old child. Each person was asked whether they agreed with:

1) Everything we learn is permanently stored in the mind, although sometimes particular details are not accessible. With hypnosis, or other special techniques, these inaccessible details could eventually be recovered; OR

2) Some details that we learn may be permanently lost from memory. Such details would never be able to be recovered by hypnosis, or any other special technique, because these details are simply no longer there.

They were also encouraged to offer comments supporting their choice.

I found that about three-quarters of these individuals chose answer number one — that is, they indicated a belief that information in long-term memory is there, but cannot be retrieved. Most of the rest chose answer number two; a few people could not make a choice.

Why do so many people believe in the permanence of memory? The most common reason is some personal experience usually involving the recovery of an idea about which the person had not thought for quite some time. For example, one person wrote: "Sometimes I will have a thought, out of nowhere, about a person whom I have not thought about for a long long time." Another wrote: "Just this past week, I was reading a book about Japan and I began thinking about the trip I took there a long time ago. I remembered the time I took a taxi to the Mitsukoshi Department Store. Then I took a walk down Ginza Street and saw some of the finest shops I'd ever seen before. It has been years since I thought about that trip and it seemed that I could remember it as if it were yesterday." A third person: "I've experienced and heard too many descriptions of spontaneous recoveries of ostensibly quite trivial memories which seem to have been triggered by just the right set of a person's experiences."

In spontaneous memory recovery, facts or details that appear to have been forgotten reappear spontaneously. Spontaneous recoveries can be striking phenomena and psychologists have wished they could study them. Unfortunately, this is very difficult since the experimenter might be forced to wait for a long time before a spontaneous recovery happens. So psychologists have instead tended to do experiments in which particular cues are provided in an attempt to recover certain memories. Typically some material is given to subjects who are then asked to recall it. Those given cues generally recall more than those who are not. But when people who were not originally given the cues later received them, they too could recall additional material. The additional material must have been stored in memory, but it could not be retrieved without a special retrieval cue. In other words, the material was available in memory, but not accessible. Experiments such as these indicate that retrieval cues are instrumental in eliciting desired material from memory. Such recovery, whether spontaneous or prompted, constitutes evidence for some people that memories are stored permanently.

Occasionally people supported their belief in permanence with reference to the work on electrical stimulation of the brain. It has been reported that stimulation of certain parts of the brain can lead to the recovery of a long-forgotten memory. Sometimes people offered a comment about hypnosis, or about repression, or about truth drugs, or even about reincarnation to support their belief in the permanence of memory.

Can brain stimulation, hypnosis, truth drugs, or other artificial means unlock the library of our minds? These phenomena seem to support rather impressively the belief that information, once in LTM, is permanently stored. Careful evaluation of the evidence in each case, however, raises substantial doubts. As we shall see, reports of "memories" that occur, either spontaneously or as a result of such memory probes as electrical stimulation, hypnosis, or drugs, may not be memories of actual events at all. Rather, there is good reason to believe that such reports may result from reconstruction of fragments of past experiences or constructions created at the time of report that bear little or no resemblance to past experience. The unlocked memories prove as subject to distortion as memories naturally recalled.

Artificial Memories: The Cues

No one would deny that it is possible to recover memories that appear to have been forgotten. This happens. But it does not constitute evidence that *all* memories are recoverable. It is plausible that we have some memories that are recoverable and other memories that are not. When something happens in life, we generally store fragments of the experience in memory. It is reasonable that some of these fragments may be altered by new experiences that we have later on.

Most of the anecdotes that suggest impressive persistence of memory never receive any independent verification. In cases in which there have been attempts to verify a memory, sometimes an actual event matches recollection, but other times the verification reveals that people are generating not memories of true events but fanciful guesses, fantasies, or plain confabulations.

This sort of phenomenon has been demonstrated in studies where people are shown films of everyday events. Later on, the people get some new information about the event, usually presented in a fairly subtle way. For example, after looking at a film of a traffic accident, people have been asked a question such as: "How fast was the car going when it ran the *stop sign*?" or "How fast was the *white sports car* going when it passed the *barn* while traveling along the *country road*?"[8] People who are asked questions that mention these objects or details later come to tell you that they have actually seen those objects or remembered those details. People will say that they saw the stop sign or saw the barn, when the stop sign was really a yield sign and no barn existed at all. This seems to happen because the information in the questions, whether true or false, can become integrated into the person's recollection of the event, thereby supplementing that memory.

But the new information can do more than add to a recollection. It can also alter or transform the recollection. In a clear demonstration of this sort of transformation, people looked at a series of slides depicting successive stages in an accident involving an automobile and a pedestrian. A red auto was traveling along a side street toward an intersection at which there was a stop sign for half of the traffic and a yield sign for the remaining traffic. The slides showed the auto turning right and knocking down a pedestrian who was crossing at the crosswalk.

After looking at the slides, everyone answered some questions about them. Some people were asked, "Did another car pass the red car while it was stopped at the stop sign?" Others were asked the same question with the words *stop sign* replaced by *yield sign.* This means that some people got a question with correct information while others got a question with incorrect information. Later, people were tested for their memory of the sign that they had seen. The correct information helped their memory. But, interestingly, the incorrect information hurt. In one case, over 80 percent of the people who got incorrect information were wrong on the final test. They told us they had seen the slide that corresponded to what they had been told rather than what they had actually seen.

In one final case, people saw a film of an accident and then answered some questions, including: "About how fast were the cars going when they smashed into each other?" The people came back a week later and answered a few more questions, one of which was "Did you see any broken glass?" There was no broken glass in the film, but those who had earlier heard the word *smashed* were more likely to tell us that they had seen the nonexistent broken glass.

Why does this happen? As we go through life we take in information from our environment. After an accident, we might take in some fragments from the experience. When an investigator comes along and asks: "About how fast were the cars going when they smashed into each other?" a new piece of information is supplied; namely, that the cars "smashed" into each other. When these two pieces of information are integrated, the person has a memory of an accident that was more severe than in fact it was. Since broken glass is associated with a severe accident, the person is more likely to "remember" that broken glass existed.

Demonstrations like these tell us that false information can be introduced into a person's recollection. It can add to the memory (as in the case of the barn) or it can actually transform the memory (as in the case of the traffic sign). Take a person who sees a stop sign, is later told it was a yield sign, and now claims to have seen a yield sign. What happened to the stop sign in memory? Certain studies that we might conduct could illuminate the issue of whether the details stored at the time of the event are in memory but simply temporarily unavailable or whether they are truly altered by information that comes in later. These studies could convincingly show that the original event remained intact. Any technique that pulled the original stop sign out of memory would tell us that it has been there. But studies cannot *prove* that an alteration has occurred and the original memory has been destroyed.

Suppose we used the strongest possible technique to induce a person to produce a particular memory. If the person failed to do so, we have not proved that the original memory is altered, for it can always be argued that we have not used a sufficiently strong technique. However, if we try every available technique to get at the original memory, and all of them fail to work, it would be reasonable to speculate that the original memory may have been altered. This position would be at least as plausible as the speculation that the memory is there but temporarily unavailable.

Psychologists have tried inventing strong techniques for digging deep into memory. In some cases nothing has worked. In these studies, an individual sees one object, say a stop sign, and is made to believe that he or she saw another object, say a yield sign. During a later test, pictures containing the two different signs have been shown and many people pick the yield sign. These people choose the sign that they heard about later, even though the truth — the true sign — is staring them in the face. Paying people in order to motivate them to do better does not seem to help. People who were offered as much as twenty-five dollars for a correct response still stuck to the sign that they heard about after the event was over. Other psychological tricks similarly failed to produce the original memory.

Even hypnosis, thought by many to have special powers in terms of getting at buried memories, doesn't work. Psychologist Bill Putnam showed people a videotape of an accident involving a car and a bicycle. Afterward some people were hypnotized while others were not. The hypnotized people were told that under hypnosis it would be possible for them to see the entire accident again just as clearly as they had seen it the first time, only this time they would be able to slow it down or zoom in on details if they chose to. But the hypnotized people made more errors and were more susceptible to leading questions than their unhypnotized counterparts. The study showed that hypnosis does not reduce retrieval difficulties; it does not allow people to retrieve a true memory. Quite the contrary, people appear to be more suggestible in the hypnotic state and more easily influenced. Suggesting some detail, like a license plate, when it could not possibly have been seen, not only induced hypnotized people to say they had seen it, but also led them to offer partial descriptions of the license number. One person said it was a California plate beginning with W or V, and this obviously made-up information was not given under any duress. Suggesting another detail, that the major character's hair was blond when it was actually black, caused hypnotized people to "remember" blond hair. Showing these people the videotape again upset them. One person said, "It's really strange because I still have the blond girl's face in my mind and it doesn't correspond to her [pointing to the woman on the videotape]. . . . It was really weird."

In sum, many attempts to pull out an original memory after it seems to have been changed have failed. This could mean that the memory can be altered or transformed by events that take place after the memory has originally been stored. New information to which a person is exposed seems to replace irrevocably the original information in the person's brain. This means that many of our memories are quite fragile. Whenever a memory for an event is called to consciousness, the potential appears to be there for substitution or alteration to occur. Memory seems not to be permanent. Rather, we have a mechanism for updating memory that sometimes leaves the original memory intact, but sometimes does not.

When does the original memory stay and when does it go? This depends completely on the type of memory. Most people know that Jacqueline Onassis was once named Jacqueline Kennedy. We did not lose the original information when we learned the new name. But this is because in our society many women undergo a name change in accord with their marital status. Our memory "knows" that it is possible to have an old name and a new name for any given individual. But, in many circumstances in life, it is logically impossible for an object to have two properties simultaneously. An automobile that was involved in an accident stopped at either a stop sign or a yield sign, but it did not stop at both. A shirt worn by a thief was not simultaneously green and yellow. In such instances, the most economical procedure may be to dismiss one memory in favor of another, much as a computer programmer will irrevocably destroy an old program instruction when a new one is created.

The implication of the notion of nonpermanent memory should give pause to all who rely on obtaining a "truthful" version of an event from someone who has in the past experienced that event. Clinical psychologists, counselors, and psychiatrists who use the amnesic interview to gain information about the prior events in someone's life typically do so to be able to make intelligent decisions about what kind of help should be given. Anthropologists, sociologists, and some experimental psychologists query people about their past in the course of studying some particular problem of interest to social science. It is important to realize that the statements made during these interviews may not be particularly accurate as reports of prior events. The contents of the interview may not reflect a person's earlier experiences and attitudes so much as their current picture of the past. It may not be possible, in some instances, ever to discover from interviews with people what actually happened in their past. Not only might the originally acquired memory depart from reality in some systematic way, but the memory may be continually subject to change after it is initially stored.

Brain Stimulation

Probably the most impressive evidence for the notion of permanent memory comes from the reports that events long forgotten are vividly recalled during electrical stimulation of certain regions of the human brain. Wilder Penfield, who is best known for this work, was operating on epileptic patients during the 1940s, removing the damaged areas in their brains in order to cure their epilepsy.[9] To guide him in pinpointing the damage, he stimulated the surface of the brain with a weak electric current in hopes of discovering, in each patient, an area in the brain that was related to the epileptic attacks. During this electrical invasion of their brains, Penfield discovered that when he moved his stimulating electrode near a portion of the brain called the hippocampus, some patients re-experienced events from their past life.

Here is an example that reached millions of Americans through *The New York Times* in 1977:

> One of Penfield's patients was a young woman. As the stimulating electrode touched a spot on her temporal lobe, she cried out: "I think I heard a mother calling her little boy somewhere. It seemed to be something that happened years ago . . . in the neighborhood where I live." Then the electrode was moved a little and she said, "I hear voices. It is late at night, around the carnival somewhere — some sort of traveling circus. I just saw lots of big wagons that they use to haul animals in." There can be little doubt that Wilder Penfield's electrodes were arousing activity in the hippocampus, within the temporal lobe, jerking out distant and intimate memories from the patient's stream of consciousness.[10]

It is of interest to examine Penfield's original writings. In his 1969 work, he seems to suggest a belief in the relatively permanent nature of memory:

> It is clear that the neuronal action that accompanies each succeeding state of consciousness leaves its permanent imprint on the brain. The imprint, or record, is a trail of facilitation of neuronal connections that can be followed again by an electric current many years later with no loss of detail, as though a tape recorder had been receiving it all.

> Consider now what happens in normal life. For a short time, a man can recall all the detail of his previous awareness. In minutes, some of it has faded beyond the reach of his command. In weeks, all of it seems to have disappeared, as far as voluntary recall is concerned, ex-

cept what seemed to him important or wakened in him emotion. But the detail is not really lost. During the subconscious interpretation of later contemporary experience, that detail is still available. This is a part of what we may call perception.[11]

Penfield apparently bases these conclusions on his observation of "flashback" responses:

> The flashback responses to electrical stimulation are altogether different. They bear no relation to present experience in the operating room. Consciousness for the moment is doubled, and the patient can discuss the phenomenon. If he is hearing music, he can hum in time to it. The astonishing aspect of the phenomenon is that suddenly he is aware of all that was in his mind during an earlier strip of time. It is the stream of a former consciousness flowing again. If music is heard, it may be orchestra or voice or piano. Sometimes he is aware of all he was seeing at the moment; sometimes he is aware only of the music. It stops when the electrode is lifted. It may be repeated (even many times) if the electrode is replaced without too long a delay. This electrical recall is completely at random. Most often, the event was neither significant nor important.[12]

Wilder Penfield's stimulating electrode captured the imagination of psychologists and has provided one of the most vivid pieces of evidence for the contention that memories are stable and permanent — a theory that might be dubbed the videorecorder model. But let us look more closely at what Penfield actually did, and what he found.

He started off with about eleven hundred patients, most of whom suffered from seizures. Typically, these people were given a local anesthetic before exploratory stimulation was carried out in order to locate the damaged areas of the brain. On the route to discovering these critical areas, some patients apparently had long-forgotten memories revived. But Penfield himself said that this "memory" response occurred in at most only forty cases — that is, only 3.5 percent of the time.[13] Thus, these "memory" responses produced by the stimulating electrode were relatively rare.

In an article written for the journal *Brain*, Penfield reviewed each one of these cases. There were eighteen men and twenty-two women. It turns out that many of these forty people claimed to hear nothing more than some music or some people singing. Only a handful said anything that indicated they had an experience even remotely resembling a real memory. And even with this handful, a closer look at exactly what the patients said during surgery reveals that real memories were not being revived, but rather the patients were "constructing" memories that did not necessarily correspond to any real experience. For example, take the patient who said, ". . . I think I heard a mother calling her little boy somewhere. It seemed to be something that happened years ago." She said it was "somebody in the neighborhood where I live." When the same spot was stimulated eighteen minutes later, she said, "Yes, I hear the same familiar sounds, it seems to be a woman calling. The same lady. That was not in the neighborhood. It seemed to be at the lumberyard." She added that she had never in her life been around a lumberyard.[14] When a patient under stimulation seems to recall people in locations in which she has never been, there is a clear indication that the individual is not "reliving" the experience but making new creations that may be in part based on memories, in that same way that we do in our dreams. A noted cognitive psychologist, Ulric Neisser, came to the same conclusions about the brain stimulation work:

> In short, the content of these experiences is not surprising in any way. It seems entirely comparable to the content of dreams, which are generally admitted to be synthetic constructions and not literal recalls. Penfield's work tells us nothing new about memory.[15]

A hint as to what might go into these reconstructions is provided by a study in which individual cases were examined in great detail. In one case the patient was a twenty-seven-year-old housewife who had a history of over five years of seizures. She entered the hospital in search of help. Her doctors tried to locate the damaged portions of the brain, the portions that were responsible for her seizures. During the course of this exploration, the woman seemed to experience what Penfield might have called revivals of memory. But on closer examination, it turned out that the content of these "memories" was simply the thought or conversation that happened to occur just before and at the time of stimulation. A direct connection could be made between what the patient said during stimulation and what was said in a discussion that had taken place within the two minutes before stimulation.[16]

In short, although Penfield would have us believe that the stimulation of the brain causes actual memories to surface to the conscious mind, the sketchy utterances of the patients do not show that they were reliving past experiences, thus casting suspicion on Penfield's "remarkable record."

Hypnosis

Since the eighteenth century, hypnosis has been studied extensively. At one time people thought hypnosis was a form of sleep. Later it was believed to be a state of narrowly focused attention in which the hypnotized person somehow becomes extremely suggestible.

A person who is in a deep hypnotic trance can be made to act as if his or her sensory inputs have been totally cut off. People can be made to see things, smell things, and hear things that aren't physically present. While under hypnosis, people can learn a lot of facts with apparent ease and can also recall past events in their lives with what seems to be surprising clarity. Each one of us is suggestible to some extent, although the exact amount depends on such different factors as the situation we find ourselves in and our ability to become deeply involved in imaginative experiences.[17]

Since the early 1960s, various U.S. law enforcement agencies have used hypnosis as an aid to criminal investigation. There are those who believe that it gives utterly fantastic results. Many of these successes have been reported in a recent book by Eugene Block called *Hypnosis: A New Tool in Crime Detection.* Here, for example, the reader will learn how hypnosis was used by the Israeli National Police Force in solving or helping to solve scores of cases. When terrorists bombed the Nahariya–Haifa bus in 1973, the driver was questioned about any suspicious passengers. He could remember nothing — until he was hypnotized. Then he was able to describe a suspicious rider with a brown paper parcel under his arm. Using this information as a lead, the Israeli police eventually caught the terrorists. Also in Block's book are descriptions of the successful role that hypnosis played in other cases, for example, in finding the Boston Strangler, the San Francisco cable car nymphomaniac, and Cleveland's Dr. Sam Sheppard, accused of killing his pregnant wife, Marilyn.

In addition to its use in solving crime, hypnosis has been used in a variety of other exotic ways. In the mid-1950s, for example, a plane crashed and the pilot claimed he could not remember what happened for about two minutes prior to the crash.[18] Under hypnosis, the pilot revealed a great deal. First, he showed both considerable concern with relative heights and a striving for relief from anxiety. With this knowledge, Dr. Raginsky, the psychiatrist conducting the inquiry, was able to guide him under hypnosis to the area of the "clouded moments" before the crash. During the first session, he was certain that he had known the correct altitudes for the letdown but was confused about why he had not used them. He also admitted that he had trouble in using the new altimeter. In the second hypnotic session, he was able to reveal the real cause of the accident. About two or three weeks before the crash he was checked out on the use of the new Omni-Magnetic Indicator. He did not understand it because of the new colors used and the opposite swing of the needles from the direction to which he had been accustomed in the past. In fact, many pilots found this instrument difficult, and it was withdrawn by the manufacturer two weeks after the accident.

If one looks at what the "experts" are saying about hypnosis, one gets a clear impression that some of them believe it works because of the permanence of memory. For example, hypnotherapists Cheek and LeCron wrote in their book, *Clinical Hypnotherapy:*

> It seems that everything that happens to us is stored in memory in complete detail. Conscious recall is limited to a very tiny part of total memory. Regression under hypnosis can bring out completely forgotten memories. It is also possible to bring them out merely by suggesting that they will be recalled. In this situation the patient remembers but doesn't relive the event.[19]

Acceptance of the power of hypnosis has reached an audience far wider than researchers in the field. An example is the case of a thirty-eight-year-old woman whose boyfriend had been murdered. She saw it happen, but the shock — and heavy drinking — almost totally blocked her memory. She was brought to the police station where a hypnotist, speaking soothingly, explained to her that the mind is like a videotape machine. What we observe is recorded, stored in the subconscious, and available for recall through hypnosis, he said. Information that she provided, previously unreported, helped crack the case. An article reporting the events noted the enormous success that the Los Angeles police department has had with hypnosis. One spokesman said it provided valuable leads and evidence in an impressive 65 percent of the cases. He further said:

> Frequently when someone is shot, raped, beaten or otherwise attacked, he or she performs a defensive maneuver. They throw up a guard against fright, anxiety, and

other traumas. Acting on a survival instinct, they hide the hurt. Through hypnosis, we make the conscious mind passive and communicate with the subconscious to release what's buried there.[20]

In sum, many proponents of hypnosis have taken successful memory recoveries to support a version of a memory permanence hypothesis. Widespread publication of these views, along with examples in which hypnosis was apparently successful, have been passed on to laypersons through the popular press.

Some people believe that hypnosis works because of the fact that every experience a person has had in life is somehow recorded in blazingly accurate detail deep in the person's brain. Hypnosis merely opens up the floodgates and lets all these memories come gushing forth.[21] People's memories have often been compared to an ordinary onion in that the memory comes in layers, with the early memories at the center and the later memories surrounding the core. Hypnosis is thought to be able to strip away the outer layers, leaving the central core exposed.

But although hypnosis is held up by many to be the magic cure for getting at deeply buried memories, this isn't necessarily the case. Even when hypnosis does work to revive a memory that is temporarily blocked, it does not involve any awesome, mysterious power. Rather it seems that hypnosis encourages a person to relax, to cooperate, and to concentrate. In this state, people feel free to talk. What they say is on occasion a new important fact, but on other occasions nothing useful is said. All too often, totally false information comes out.

That hypnotized subjects who are asked to relive former experiences often produce a wealth of fabricated material was vividly shown by one psychologist who hypnotized college students and then regressed them back to their sixth birthday.[22] He asked them to go back in their minds to this day in order to relive the events just as they had originally occurred, and to describe exactly what had happened to them. The students gave lengthy descriptions, peppered with numerous tiny details. Unbeknownst to these students, the psychologist had gotten descriptions from the students' parents and other sources to compare with the students' memories. The result: Although the "memories" were rich in detail, they were hopelessly inaccurate. Events from other birthdays got mixed up with the events from the sixth birthday. Facts that the students had merely read about in books and magazines got included in their "memory" for their birthday. In some cases, the students made up things that never actually happened.

Some of the hypnotized students who were allegedly remembering their sixth birthday made critical mistakes. When the psychologist asked a question about the time, they looked at their wrists, even though none of them wore wrist watches when they were six. They answered questions about news events that had occurred long after they had reached the age of six. When given a test that they had actually taken when they were six years old, they could not answer the items as they had when at that early age. They knew too much.

No solid studies exist that show recall during a state of hypnosis is any more accurate or complete than recall under ordinary waking conditions. What is worse, people under hypnosis have been known to "recall" events from their past confidently and to fabricate future scenarios with the same confidence. The *American Bar Association Journal* expressed its nervousness with the use of hypnosis in legal areas:

> People can flat-out lie under hypnosis, and the examiner is no better equipped to detect the hypnotic lie than any other kind. Even more serious, a willing hypnotic subject is more pliable than he normally would be, more anxious to please his questioner. Knowing even a few details of an event, often supplied in early contacts with police, may provide the subject with enough basis to create a highly

detailed 'memory' of what transpired, whether he was there or not.[23]

Truth Serum

Throughout history, the belief has been held that certain drugs could strip away the chaff in memory and force a person to speak the truth. An ancient Chinese test required a suspected wrongdoer to chew rice powder during an interrogation; the suspect then spit out the powder, and if it was dry, he was condemned. In Aztec Mexico, it was believed that peyote cactus (which contains mescaline) conferred the "power of second sight." This power could help in discovering the identity of a thief or in recovering stolen property. More recently in times of war, prisoners have been forced to take certain narcotic drugs to assist in their interrogation. And modern therapy has included the use of sodium pentathol and similar drugs to assist patients in talking about things that trouble them. This technique, sometimes called narcoanalysis, proved useful for treating emotional casualties in wartime. Even the usually noncommunicative patient would talk freely under the influence of these drugs.

Truth drugs have also been used by police investigators to facilitate the interrogation of suspects and witnesses to crimes. A person who has been accused of a crime is often desperate for some sort of corroborating evidence to support his or her innocence. Many have been tempted to submit to being questioned while drugged. To force someone to submit involuntarily to such an examination is, of course, repugnant, but voluntary examination in a drugged condition is not. In the early 1920s a physician in Dallas, Texas, tried using a drug called scopolamine for interrogating suspected criminals. He interviewed two prisoners at the Dallas County Jail, both of whom received injections, and both of whom denied the charges against them. At their trial, they were found not guilty. Enthusiastic about his results, the physician remarked that under the drug a person "cannot create a lie . . . and there is no power to think or reason."[24]

In another investigation, two doctors attempted to get information from patients — all soldiers — who were known to have committed serious crimes, but who refused to admit it. The doctors used one of the so-called truth drugs, sodium amytal, to try to get these people to confess. Five of them were accused of robbery, ranging from thefts of butter for sale on the black market to theft of an automobile, and five were drug addicts who had illegal access to narcotics. One of them had been accused of molesting women and young children, while two were allegedly guilty of homicidal assault. They steadfastly insisted they were innocent of the charges.

After the drug had been injected into a vein, the soldiers felt sleepy, but could speak. Their speech was typically thick, mumbling, and disconnected. The interrogator's questions depended on the patient's individual history and attitude. One trick that was used was to pretend that the patient had already confessed and urge him to elaborate details he had "already described." Nine individuals confessed. Even those who did not confess gave some information which had previously been withheld from other investigators.[25]

Why did these soldiers confess while under the influence of the drug? Many explanations have been advanced. One of the most reasonable is that the drug diminishes the person's caution and restricts the desire for self-preservation. Sometimes people strongly want to confess but cannot bring themselves to do it. The drug gives them an excuse. Another explanation is that the drug has some special ability to strip away any conscious control and lay bare the "truth."

The evidence looks impressive at first blush. But the soldiers who remembered many "true" facts also "remembered" many false ones. Several of the soldiers revealed fantasies, fears, and delusions that approached the quality of delirium and could readily be distinguished from reality by their fantastic quality. At times, however, the examiner was simply unable to distinguish the truth from the fantasy. The two doctors who studied these soldiers urged caution in interpreting the evidence. They explicitly stated that "testimony concerning dates and specific places is untrustworthy and often contradictory," that "names and events are of questionable veracity." Furthermore, "contradictory statements are often made without the patient actually trying to conceal the truth, but succeeding in this by his confusion between what has actually happened and what he thinks or fears may have happened."[26]

A good example of this is the soldier P. V., who was accused of being involved in a robbery of the Post Exchange. At first he denied having been present at the actual scene of the robbery, but later described plausible details of "what happened" the night the Post Exchange was robbed. A subsequent investigation revealed that the soldier had not been a direct accomplice, but had bought goods from the men who had committed the robbery. His description of the details of the crime was a reconstruction of second-hand information and pure fantasy. Numerous observations of reconstructions such as this one make it hard to believe in any supposed power of truth drugs. At the end of their report, the doctors express their beliefs: "There is no such thing as a 'truth serum.' "

So-called truth drugs have also been used in psychiatric interviews, for example to aid a patient's recollection of traumatic experiences. The drugs are popular because they are easy to give, have few unpleasant side effects, and have a dramatic effect on a patient. Typically, the body relaxes immediately. A few people become momentarily excited, silly and giggly, but this passes and the person falls into a state that is similar to what you feel when you have just awakened from a deep sleep. The drugs then seem to relieve the patient from the anxiety and guilt that block good communication. But the two medical officers who made the most extensive use of the technique concluded that in almost all cases they could obtain essentially the same material and emotional release in the course of therapy without using any drugs at all.

Another prominent psychiatrist who has used sodium amytal extensively in investigating the personalities of men accused of various antisocial acts does not seem to have much faith in its ability to get at the truth. The people he talked with ranged from those with character disorders and neuroses to psychotics. They had been charged with offenses that ranged from mild delinquency to murder. Even after hours of interrogation with a person in a drugged condition, the psychiatrist did not feel that he knew the objective reality any better. He still had no idea whether a given antisocial act had or had not occurred. The drugs seemed to be useless for getting at some underlying truth: "Guilt-ridden subjects under sedation were prone to confess to offenses they had imagined in fantasy but had not in fact committed. Psychopathic individuals could, to the point of unconsciousness, deny crimes that every objective sign indicated they had committed."[27]

Other studies with "normal" people have shown that it is relatively easy for people to maintain a lie despite injections of a truth drug. In one case, subjects revealed shameful and guilt-producing episodes of their past life and then invented false self-protective stories to cover up these episodes. They were injected with sodium amytal and subjected to rigorous cross-examination on their cover stories. The results showed that normal people with no overtly pathological traits could stick to their invented stories and not confess. On the other hand, neurotic individuals tended to confess more easily, but often to offenses that they had never committed.

In sum, it appears that people can withhold information and lie despite the drug. More dangerously, some individuals are so suggestible that they will describe — especially in response to suggestive questioning — behavior that never in fact occurred. The drugs may facilitate access to psychological reality, but they do not seem to be useful in getting at the facts.

4
What Causes Forgetting: The Imperfect Mechanism

One day a young woman forgot something very important. She was so distraught that she dashed off a letter to "Dear Abby":

Dear Abby:

My fiancé Joey and I are having a cold war because of what he refers to as a "Freudian slip." The other night in the middle of a warm embrace, I called him "Jimmy." (Jimmy was my former boyfriend.)

Needless to say, I was terribly embarrassed and tried my best to convince Joey that I was NOT thinking of Jimmy. I honestly wasn't, Abby. I went with Jimmy for a long time, but I can truthfully say that I have absolutely no feelings for him anymore, and I love Joey with all my heart.

How does something like this happen? Is it really just a slip of the tongue, or is there something in my subconscious that is driving me to destroy a good relationship with someone I love by driving him away with a slip of the tongue?

Please help me. My future relationship with Joey hinges on your reply. Thank you. Sign me . . .

— I HATE FREUD

Abby answered:

Dear Hate:

Not every slip of the tongue has a subconscious symbolic meaning, and not every accident conceals a wish to get hurt. As Freud himself said, "Sometimes a cigar is just a cigar!"

Your slip of the tongue does not necessarily signify a continuing attachment to your ex-boyfriend, but could simply reflect a strongly conditioned habitual response stemming from your association with him over a long period of time.

Forgetting can be embarrassing. No matter how educated a person might be, practically no one is free from this experience. Some years back, two English psychologists made a recording of a discussion that took place at the Cambridge Psychological Society. A couple of weeks later, they wrote to all the psychologists who had attended and asked them to write down all they could recall about the discussion. The reports that came in were checked against the recorded version. The comparisons were striking. The average number of specific points recalled by any individual was barely more than 8 percent of the total recorded. Furthermore, almost half of the remembered points were substantially incorrect. Events were reported that had never taken place at all. Happenings were remembered that had taken place on some other occasion and were incorrectly recalled as having occurred at this particular discussion. Errors and confusions seemed to be the rule rather than the exception.[1]

Forgetting is a common experience for all of us. This probably accounts for the stupendous success of Lorayne and Lucas's *The Memory Book*, which swept the country in 1974 and 1975. *The Memory Book* is a practical book filled with tricks to help you remember grocery lists, playing cards, names to go with faces, and anything else you do not want to forget. It advertises that "you can remember all the things that make the vital difference in your everyday existence, eliminating the unnecessary loss of so much knowledge and information that should be yours to keep and use forever."[2] These techniques seem to work, at least for some people. But why are they needed in the first place? What causes forgetting?

One of the first experimental investigations into forgetting was conducted by a nineteenth-century German named Hermann Ebbinghaus in 1885. Since there were no large pools of subjects available when he was doing his research, he used himself as his sole subject. When Ebbinghaus was in his thirties, he memorized stanzas of *Don Juan*. About twenty years later, during his mid-fifties, he tried to relearn the stanzas. Despite the feeling that he had completely forgotten them, he learned them much faster the second time. To Ebbinghaus, this savings in relearning time indicated that at least some of the initial learning had been retained.

As Ebbinghaus wanted to study forgetting in its purest possible form, unaffected by any previous learning or emotional factors, he invented the nonsense syllable. Nonsense syllables are composed of three letters, usually with a vowel in the middle, such as DAX, COL, or FUP. In one of his many experiments, Ebbinghaus learned a list of thirteen syllables well enough so that he could repeat the list without making mistakes. He kept track of how long it took him to do this. After an interval during which forgetting could take place, he learned the list a second time, again keeping track of the time. The difference between the amount of time it took to learn the list in the two cases was his measure of forgetting.

Ebbinghaus worked with many different lists, sometimes relearning them an hour later, sometimes a day, sometimes six days. He came up with the graph shown opposite, which has since become very famous and is called the "forgetting curve." It basically indicates that while we forget a good deal of new information soon after we learn it, forgetting then becomes more gradual. This curve has been reproduced by many other researchers since Ebbinghaus, using not only nonsense syllables, but a variety of other materials as well.

Why We Forget

Ebbinghaus never had much to say on the subject of why forgetting occurs. Forgetting occurs in many ways and undoubtedly for many reasons. One reason we forget is that we never stored the information we want to remember in the first place. Because we didn't pay enough attention to it, it was lost from our memory system in a matter of seconds. But even in cases where we seemingly have learned something quite well, we are sometimes unable to remember it later. Psychologists have advanced a number of reasons for this.

Interference

One theory of why people forget events they have experienced is that other events prevent the original one from being remembered. In other words, events interfere with each other in memory. Since most of us are fairly active human beings, it is likely that we encounter numerous events that potentially interfere with others we may wish to remember.

If interference is the problem, then we ought to be able to eliminate forgetting by eliminating interfering events. One way to accomplish this might be to go to sleep immediately

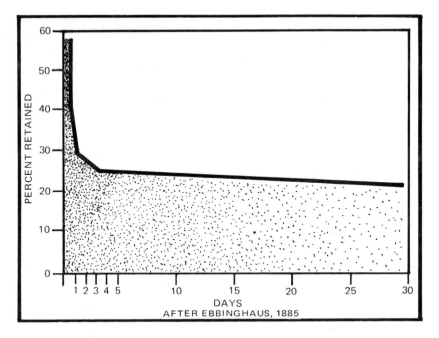

The forgetting process: Initially the curve dips sharply; then it flattens out.

after learning new material. This is exactly what was done in a classic experiment performed over fifty years ago.[3] Only two subjects were used, each of whom had to learn some new information. One of the subjects went to sleep immediately after learning. The other carried on normal activities of eating, studying, swimming, or whatever. After some time had passed, the subjects were asked to recall what they had learned. Their forgetting curves are shown on the following page; they indicate without a doubt that the subject who slept remembered better than the one who remained awake. This observation prompted the investigators to remark that "forgetting is not so much a matter of the decay of old impressions and association as it is a matter of interference, inhibition, or obliteration of the old by the new."

Another clever technique to eliminate interfering events

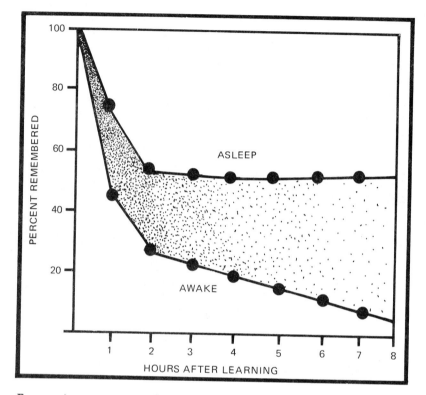

Forgetting curves: asleep and awake

and slow forgetting can be uniquely illustrated with cockroaches. If you wrap up a cockroach so that it gets lots of body
contact, it will become immobile for as long as two hours.
Presumably this blocks out interfering events. With this in
mind, two psychologists did a study using two groups of
cockroaches. The insects were first taught to avoid a corner of
their cage by shocking them every time they went to the
corner. Afterward, one group was immobilized while a second
group was allowed to roam around the cage freely engaging in
whatever activity cockroaches normally engage in. The insects were then tested to see how well they remembered to
avoid the corner of the cage. Those that stayed awake did
much worse, presumably because of the interference pro-

duced by their other activities. Like the subjects who went to sleep, the cockroaches who hibernated remembered better.[4]

Retrieval Failure

A key process in remembering something is being able to retrieve it. We often search our giant warehouse of knowledge without being able to find what we want. The importance of good retrieval was shown in a study in which people looked at a picture very briefly. They were asked to describe what they had seen, including as many details as they possibly could remember, and at the same time to make drawings of the picture. At first, people could not remember very many details, remembering little more than a man, a truck, a boardwalk, and a storefront. The subjects were then asked to think hard about what they had seen and to "free associate" to their memory of the picture. They spoke aloud any words that happened to come to mind, continuing with their thinking until as many as 120 associations had been produced. Then they were asked to recall the picture again. This time, they reported many details that had not been mentioned earlier, indicating that they had stored in memory considerably more information about the picture than they were able to produce initially. Free association seemed to supply them with new clues that aided their retrieval process and enabled them to remember more. More popularly, this is known as "jogging one's memory."

Sometimes we have the feeling that even though we can't quite remember some fact, it is on the tip of our tongues and that with just the right cue it would surface. In a now-famous study conducted to understand a bit more about the "tip-of-the-tongue," or TOT, phenomenon, university students were given definitions of uncommon English words and told to find a word in their memory that fit each definition.[5] For example, when given the definition "A navigational instrument used for measuring angular distances," the person was to come up with the word *sextant*. Since the words used were unusual ones, such as *zealot, exculpate,* and *sampan,* there were many instances in which people could not find the word at all. However, on two hundred occasions students claimed the word was on the tip of the tongue.

While in the TOT state, people would often think of words other than the correct one. The words they thought of usually had a similar sound. When trying to remember *sampan*, for example, some real words such as *Saipan, Siam, Cheyenne,* and *sarong* came to mind. Some made-up words such as *sanching* and *sympoon* also came to mind.

Interestingly enough, in over half of these TOT occasions when the word would simply not come, people could still correctly guess the first letter of the word they were seeking. They also seemed to know something about the last letter of the word and how many syllables the word contained. This means that people can remember certain aspects of a word even though they cannot produce the whole thing. Remembering may therefore occur a little at a time.

The same sort of bit-by-bit retrieval happens when people recognize a familiar face and try to remember the name that goes with it. The experience of seeing someone we recognize but cannot name is common. A psychologist wrote about this in a paper called "I Recognize Your Face but I Can't Remember Your Name."[6] Subjects in this study were shown pictures of famous people and asked to recall their names. Whenever a subject was unable to think of the name, but felt sure that he knew it and that it was on the verge of coming back, he was considered to be in the TOT state. Some of the faces were those of entertainers (such as Cary Grant and Carol Burnett), while others were artists (such as Pablo Picasso) or politicians (such as Spiro Agnew). Some of the faces were easy for people to name, while others were more difficult. One movie star, Ann Margaret, for example, was mistaken by different subjects for Marilyn Monroe, Jayne Mansfield, Tuesday Weld, or Lana Turner.

In over six hundred instances, subjects were in the TOT state. In all cases, they pressed on in their search for the correct name. One of the interesting things noticed was that when subjects tried to remember a person's name, they first tried to locate his profession and then tried to remember where they most likely had seen the person. For example, one subject who was trying to remember the name Elliot Gould said, "He is a movie star, latest film was *Bob, Carol, Ted and Alice."* Another who was searching for a name to attach to the picture of Arthur Godfrey said, "He was in show business and is seen in newspapers."

While trying to remember a person's name, other information such as initial letters or number of syllables in the name was also available, but tended to be used later in the search. Thus, one person who was looking for the name Liza Minnelli first tried out the names Monetti, Mona, Magetti, Spaghetti, and Bogette.

Studies of the tip-of-the-tongue experience indicate that memory retrieval is an extremely complex process. A person can retrieve a word or name by using sounds or by using lots of different kinds of related information. Stored with each word or name, then, must be associations or pathways to other words and sounds. Words and events are also associated with each other, and these associations can be of great help in the search for a correct word or name.

Thus, if I showed you a photograph of a well-known person and you could not immediately remember his name, you might try to "get there" through other things that you know about him. If you realized that you saw him on the evening news last week, then the name Walter Cronkite might very easily pop into your mind.

Motivated Forgetting

People who return from a vacation often tend to remember the happy times and forget the sad times. People who gamble are prone to remember the times they won and to forget the times they lost. This has led to a belief that we deliberately forget because we want to forget.

Much of the evidence for motivated forgetting comes

from individual cases. One example concerned a college professor, Dr. R. J., who lost her memory. To their shock, her friends and family found that she would look into their eyes without the faintest glimpse of recognition. She couldn't remember where she lived and recognized almost no one. She couldn't remember her own name or anything about what she did for a living:

> But she did remember clearly all she knew about English literature, enough so that she was able to teach again even before the rest of her memory returned. To their dismay, her students, even the ones she had been very close to, were also forgotten. That is, she could not recall their names, details about their backgrounds, grades, or specific information that linked them to her past. But curiously, she had an "emotional memory" for them and for other people she had liked very much or disliked strongly. She was a woman of strong opinions who tended to overreact to people and causes. She would say to previous friends, "I'm sorry I don't know who you are, but for some reason I like you (or feel safe around you, or can trust you)." On the other hand, encounters with previous adversaries might bring a blush of guilt or a moment of fear as she would hesitatingly report how silly she felt reacting so strongly at first meeting the "stranger." She was even a bit ashamed at "judging a book by its cover." This was one of the few negative feelings in her otherwise euphoric state of amnesia.
>
> R. J. gradually pieced her life together again, with a little help from her friends. They reminded her, for example, that she had usually been on a diet and had not enjoyed eating as much as she did now since she was a chubby teenager. (She went back on her diet.) They informed her that she need not keep doing dishes by hand because she had a dishwasher. Once so reminded, she recalled how to operate it. But the more she remembered,

the less happy R. J. became. It seems that she had suffered an incredible series of traumatic events within the past year climaxing with the breakup of her marriage and the sudden death of her mother before her eyes. Amnesia put all that past ugliness, and more, out of awareness. In its place this motivated forgetting had given her peace of mind. But it was too upsetting to the rest of us to have someone in our midst who didn't remember what she was supposed to.⑦

Eventually, R. J. was able to remember all of her traumatic experiences; when they returned, so did all of her other lost memories. Even though the return of her memories made her wiser, she was also much sadder. More than most of us ever will, R. J. understood the true meaning in Christina Rossetti's words in *Remember:* "Better by far you should forget and smile than that you should remember and be sad."

Motivated forgetting is very likely the cause of Edward Kennedy's poor memory of the events of Chappaquiddick. That summer weekend in 1969, Kennedy joined a group of campaign workers at a reunion cookout in a small cottage on Chappaquiddick Island. Sometime after 11 P.M., Kennedy slipped away from the group in order to catch the last ferry; Mary Jo Kopechne was with him. Kennedy missed the correct road and instead turned right down a dirt lane called Dike Road. Crossing a narrow wooden bridge, Kennedy's car flipped over into the water. Kennedy managed to swim to safety but his companion did not.

For years afterward, the press hounded Kennedy for information. Five years after the incident, he told reporters for the Boston *Globe*, "I wish I could help you. . . . I don't recall that. . . . I have no recollection. . . . That is the best I can give you. . . . I have no memory. . . . I really couldn't tell you."[8] While some would call this "the model of the stonewall," there is no need to assume this. After such an enormously stressful experience, many individuals wish to forget . . . and often their wish is granted.

Memory Never Stored

We must never underestimate one of the most obvious reasons for forgetting, namely, that the information was never stored in memory in the first place. This could happen for a number of reasons: The thing we wish to remember didn't last long enough for us to absorb it; it lasted long enough but we didn't notice it; or we noticed it but didn't pay sufficient attention to ensure it would make its way into long-term memory. People would be surprised at how little knowledge they have about even the most common everyday items. Take a U.S. penny. Most people would be willing to say that they know what a penny looks like or at least that they would have no trouble recognizing one when they saw it. We've seen and handled thousands of pennies in our lifetimes. But surprisingly, people cannot reproduce a penny very accurately, cannot recall what is on it, and cannot recognize the difference between a real penny and a fake one that has been altered in simple ways.[9]

The investigators who wanted to study people's ability to remember this common object started by asking people to draw from memory what is on each side of a U.S. penny. Subjects were asked to include all details that they could. In general, the subjects performed remarkably poorly.

There are eight critical features that people could have included:

Top side	*Bottom side*
Head	Building
"IN GOD WE TRUST"	"UNITED STATES OF
"LIBERTY"	AMERICA"
Date	"E PLURIBUS UNUM"
	"ONE CENT"

Of the eight critical features, people recalled and correctly located an average of three. Only one person, an active penny collector, accurately remembered all eight.

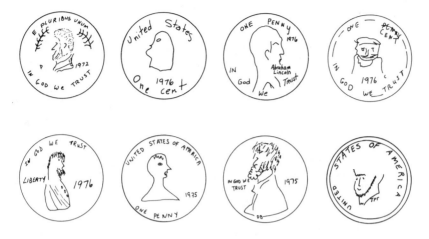

Pennies drawn from memory

In another study, subjects were given fifteen different drawings of the head of a U.S. penny. The subjects had to look at all of them and decide which was the accurate reproduction. Fewer than half of the subjects chose penny A, which is correct. A significant number of people thought that G and M were the correct pennies, even though they were counterfeits.

The subjects who participated in this study were surprised and often embarrassed by the results. Initially the task sounded so simple, but it turned out to be much more difficult. Certainly these people had seen pennies many thousands of times during their lives; some had even collected them as a hobby. Why could they not retrieve this information from memory?

One reason is that while a penny is certainly a meaningful object, the particular details that appear on it are not. We do not learn the details of a penny because there is no need for us to know them. All we need in life is to be able to distinguish a penny from other coins, which means learning its color and size. Even when we have to tell it apart from a foreign coin of a similar color and size, a gross comparison of their features will generally be sufficient. Similarly there are other common objects for which we have very incomplete and

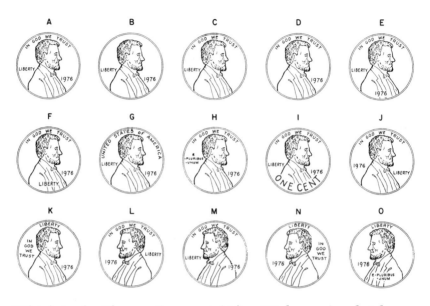

Which is the "honest" penny? (After Nickerson and Adams, 1979, p. 297)

imprecise representation in memory. To see this, simply try to draw from memory a telephone dial, a dollar bill, or some other common object.

Brand-new experiences are undoubtedly forgotten for all of these reasons. Sometimes we wish to forget, sometimes we temporarily are unable to retrieve, and sometimes interference prevents memory from emerging to consciousness. And sometimes the information was never stored to begin with. Any of these reasons can cause us to forget an isolated fact, such as what you had for breakfast yesterday or what you were doing last Tuesday at noon. But another force is also at work, namely, a constructive force. People seem to be able to take bits and pieces of their experiences and integrate them to construct objects and events that never really happened. These forces may help us to explain why some individuals perceive things that others do not.

5
Mind and Matter: Influences on Memory

In the course of our daily lives, we are constantly bombarded by external influences. We experience stressful events. We feel giddy from drinking alcohol. We age. We observe unfamiliar sights. All of these can take their toll on memory. Even sex, it is believed, can sometimes influence memory in funny ways.

Stress and Memory

Not long ago, an account was made public of the brutal treatment suffered by Venezuelan poet Ali Lameda, who was imprisoned for more than six years in North Korea but managed to survive his ordeal to tell about it. Lameda had been a member of the Venezuelan Conmunist Party when the North Korean government invited him to Korea to work as a propaganda translator in 1966. But a year later, he was arrested on charges of being a foreign agent. Lameda said that after his arrest, he was denied food, medical treatment, and any change of clothing. He was continuously interrogated in a most grueling fashion. Eventually, he was convicted and sentenced to twenty years' imprisonment with forced labor.

During his ordeal, the food was poor and the conditions extremely brutal; he lost fifty pounds. Despite the extreme unpleasantness, the poet managed to commit to memory more than four hundred poems and three hundred sonnets, some of which were published later. "They killed everything except my memory," he said.

How could the poet — when his world was crumbling around him — memorize all those poems? Was his experience a unique one? Undoubtedly, memorizing them took a great deal of concentration. But by concentrating on the poems, he was able to distract himself from his torturous situation. With mammoth effort, he rehearsed and organized his poems, thereby committing them to long-term memory. Doing so also helped him block out some of the painful happenings occurring to and around him.

Does stress, then, facilitate memory? To the contrary. Generally speaking, strongly negative and stressful emotions hinder accurate perception and memory. If a fire breaks out in a crowded theater, you will undoubtedly describe the event over and over to friends. This repeated rehearsal will improve your memory of the event itself, and perhaps also reinforce the details of your initial perception. The stress and fear that accompany such an event, however, usually result in a poorer ability to perceive accurately the details of the event and in a poorer recall ability later on. Yet Lameda's case is so dramatically opposite. The explanation — and the complete relationship between stress and memory — is captured in the Yerkes-Dodson law, a law that was named in honor of the two men who first noted it in 1908. Strong motivational states such as stress or emotional arousal facilitate learning and memory up to a point, after which there is a decrement.

In the illustration of the Yerkes-Dodson law, we see the relationship between the level of emotional arousal and effectiveness of perception and memory. At very low levels of arousal, for example when a person is just waking up in the morning, the nervous system may not be fully functioning and sensory messages may not get through. Performance is optimal at moderate levels of arousal; at high levels of arousal, performance begins to decline.

The optimum level of arousal and the exact shape of the curve depend on the kind of task a person is engaged in. A simple, well-learned habit would be much less susceptible to disruption by emotional arousal than a more complex re-

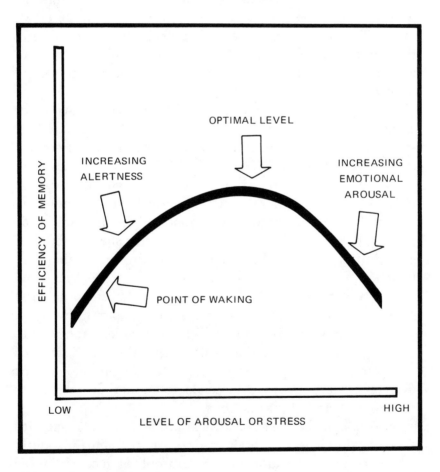

The Yerkes-Dodson law

sponse that depends upon the integration of several thought processes. In a moment of intense fear, you would probably still be able to tell someone your name, but you would have trouble playing a Beethoven sonata on the piano.

Scientists have learned about the effects of stress by watching people perform in stressful circumstances.[1] In one case, servicemen were taken on a plane flight and deceived into believing a dangerous emergency had arisen. One of the engines was turned off and the servicemen were told an emergency crash landing in the sea was probably going to be necessary because the plane's landing gear was not working. At this point, the servicemen were asked to complete two forms. The first form, which asked about the disposition of their private belongings, was given them to enhance the realism and conceal the purpose of the experiment. The second form tested retention of emergency instructions; it was explained by saying it was necessary to convince the insurance company that appropriate precautions had been taken. The stressed servicemen made many more errors than a control group of unstressed servicemen who did not believe they were in danger. In a second study, stress was induced in army recruits who were on a simulated tactical exercise and were totally isolated except for a telephone link. Some were made anxious by telling them that they were being shelled with live ammunition by mistake; others, by telling them they had mistakenly been put in an area subject to intense, accidental atomic radiation. After an army recruit had been sufficiently stressed, he was required to contact headquarters by radio. The radio, however, was broken. In order to repair it he had to follow certain complicated instructions. The study showed that simulated danger situations definitely produce a good deal of anxiety which also tends to hinder the ability to remember detailed instructions.

Although there can be ethical problems associated with exposing people to such high levels of stress, scientific inquiry occasionally necessitates it. For example, I recently asked people who were reported to have a high fear of snakes to participate in a study on memory. The subjects were warned that they might have a stuffed cobra placed in the room near them. I justified exposing people to this highly stressful situation on the grounds that a limited but safe exposure to the snake would "desensitize" them a little bit and help them overcome their abnormal fear. In the study, people were shown a film of a complex event that they had to remember later on. Some of them watched the film with the snake nearby. Others watched the film with a teddy bear nearby. All were later tested on their recollections of the film. The results were straightforward: Those whose movie companion had been a sneering stuffed cobra did much worse on the subsequent test.

Because of the ethical and moral problems of subjecting people to stress, a number of investigators have chosen to conduct their studies on people who voluntarily subject themselves to real danger in such activities as parachute jumping, rock climbing, and deep sea diving. In one case, army parachutists were asked to perform a mental task before jumping. The anxiety of the impending jump tended to interfere with performance on the task. Why does this happen? One explanation is that stress leads to a narrowing of focus. Under high stress, people concentrate on fewer features in their environment, and thus many features get less attention. So much energy is expended on anxiety that not much is left over for coping with anything else.

So far we have talked about extreme stress and arousal as factors that inhibit a person's ability to remember. These factors affect nearly all of us. But there is another kind of anxiety, a general anxiety that affects some of us more than others. Psychologists have developed standardized tests to measure a person's general level of anxiety. A colleague at the University of Washington, Judith Siegel, and I wondered whether persons who have a higher level of general anxiety would perform more poorly in a memory test than those with a lower level of general anxiety. A related question was whether a person who had undergone a number of recent life changes, such as the death of a close friend or loss of a job, would show deficits in memory. Several studies had shown that the accumulation of undesirable life changes (or life stress as it has been called) is associated with psychological problems such as anxiety and depression. Thus we thought people with a great deal of life stress might have less ability to remember recent experiences.

In the study we conducted, people were shown a series of slides depicting a pickpocket.[2] About a minute after looking at the slides, they were tested with questions such as: "The thief wore a: 1) heavy shirt; 2) long winter coat; 3) short winter coat; 4) light jacket; or 5) down vest." For each participant we had measures of general anxiety and life stress. Our results were clear: People who were generally anxious did worse on the memory test than people who were not. We also found indications that people who are experiencing great life stress also tend to perform more poorly on a test of recent memories.

This study suggests that memory is affected by a person's psychological state. High anxiety hinders memory. This is likely to be because highly anxious individuals do not pay adequate attention to important cues in their environment and thus may miss information crucial for accurate memory.

Another way in which investigators have gotten information about stress and memory is to interview people after they have witnessed disasters. Sometimes when people live through a natural disaster, such as an earthquake, flood, or fire, they often remember very little. Forces seem to operate to help people forget, especially when such forgetting would make life more bearable. This is also often the case with air crashes. In 1973, the Denver *Post* reported an incident involving a Yugoslav Airlines DC-9. A bomb planted by Croatian terrorists exploded in the plane. A stewardess named Vesna fell over thirty thousand feet from the disintegrating aircraft and survived. (She is the only person known to have survived a fall from such a height.)

Vesna suffered brain damage, a fractured spine, and paralysis from the waist down. Metal was embedded in various parts of her body. But within two years she had almost fully recovered. What did she remember? Only stepping onto the plane to start the flight. From then on, her memory is a complete blank until the time she woke up in a hospital. Doctors have been concerned about her flying again for fear that some sudden shock could bring back the entire terrifying experience. They tell her she is luckier not to remember.

More recently, survivors of another air disaster were interviewed. A Pan American jet was taxiing on an air strip on Tenerife Island in the Canary Islands when in a dense fog another jet coming down the runway collided with it. The force of the explosions that followed killed nearly six hundred people. A doctoral student from San Diego interviewed some of the sixty-four survivors five months after the accident. One man lost his wife of thirty-seven years and continues to blame himself for her death. The reason: For minutes after the accident he sat stunned and motionless, enveloped by fire and smoke. Finally he roused himself and led his wife to a jagged hole above his seat. He climbed out onto the wing and reached down and took hold of his wife's hand, but an explosion from within literally blew her out of his hands and pushed him back and down onto the wing. He stepped away from the plane, turned to go back after her, but seconds later the plane blew up.

Most of the others could not remember as much, and many suffered symptoms of traumatic neurosis. One woman claimed she ate constantly, couldn't sleep or relax, and felt her memory was affected in that she had enormous difficulty concentrating.[3]

One thing that prevents accurate memory of disastrous events is the need people have to find scapegoats to blame for destruction and loss of life.[4] This happened in the case of the Coconut Grove tragedy, a Boston nightclub fire in November, 1942, that led to the deaths of nearly five hundred people. All were trapped inside the club and died not only of burns but also of suffocation. The horror of this tragedy gave rise to an outcry to avenge the victims by finding and punishing those responsible. People became obsessed with the question of who was responsible for the incident.

The problem with this need to blame is that it draws attention away from more fundamental causes. A spotlight on the targets of blame may give the appearance that corrective action is being taken when it is not. Time spent looking for people to blame means that less time is spent discovering ways to prevent a tragedy from happening again.

Another aftermath of a disaster is that people need to understand why it occurred and what it means. Thus, people talk a lot about it among themselves. Disasters are largely shared experiences; the conversations participants have with one another can influence one another's memories. The offshoot of this is that it becomes very difficult to get a completely unbiased, accurate account of a disaster from survivors.

Brain Injuries and Memory

If a person is hit in the head or receives a brain injury in some other way, various events that occurred just before the trauma may be forgotten. Like the shock of experiencing a disaster, brain injuries can wipe out the immediate and surrounding circumstances. This is called retrograde amnesia. With retrograde amnesia, it is generally true that the more severe the trauma, the longer the period of amnesia. So a football player who is stunned by a hard tackle might forget a few seconds of his life. But a survivor of a serious automobile accident involving major head injury might forget months or even years. Fortunately, retrograde amnesia typically clears up and lost memories are recovered.

They did not clear up, however, in one unusual case. A young man called the police to say that his mother had shot herself. An ambulance responded and took the mother to the hospital. She was unconscious during the trip but soon regained consciousness and gave an articulate account of the circumstances that preceded her traumatic experience. She said she had been writing a letter and that her son came into the room. She told him, "Get away, Donald, and don't annoy me." Then there was a shot. The implication was clear that her son had shot her. The poor mother then became delirious and died, whereupon the son was charged with killing his mother.

A doctor testified at the son's trial on the workings of retrograde amnesia. He believed that the brain injury caused by the mother's self-inflicted wound had caused much of her memory of the events immediately preceding the shot to be lost. The last thing she remembered was writing a letter, which was actually done sometime before. This testimony helped to clear the defendant of the murder charge.

Electroconvulsive shock therapy (ECT) is a form of injury to the brain. The therapy has been used to treat severe psychotic illnesses, including deep depression. During a therapy session, electrodes are attached to the head and electric current is applied for as long as one second, causing a brain seizure. Within minutes the patient recovers, feeling groggy for a brief period. What is interesting is that the patients often cannot recall either the treatment or any events immediately before it — retrograde amnesia. Critics of this treatment fear that it will cause permanent brain damage, including the loss of even some distant memories. Ernest Hemingway, for example, believed that the shock treatments he received wiped out his store of experiences and ruined his writing career. However, the evidence for this tends to be anecdotal.

Injury to the brain can also cause forgetting events that occur after the trauma, a phenomenon called anterograde amnesia. For instance, a survivor of a severe auto accident may lose all memory of the hospital stay. Many who have suffered brain injuries find that contrary to our mind's normal practice of displacing earlier memories with more current ones, their memories have lost the capacity to update, to incorporate new memories. When you think about your child, it is usually as he or she looks, talks, and acts today. It may be difficult to reconstruct an image of five years ago without the aid of photographs. But one brain-injured patient who was asked to draw a woman and then a bus reproduced the style and model current ten years earlier.[5] In some ways, these people are living with memories that are not malleable.

Sex and Memory

According to a New York physician, sexual intercourse can cause sudden loss of memory that lasts for several hours. The physician had treated several patients who experienced "profound memory loss and disorientation" after sexual intercourse, and he reported these cases in the prestigious *New England Journal of Medicine*.[6]

The first case involved a sixty-four-year-old woman with high blood pressure. One day after sexual intercourse with her husband, she suddenly experienced confusion and could not recognize her surroundings. About twelve hours later, she had recovered. She worried because this was the second episode of this sort in a three-week period.

A second case involved a forty-seven-year-old man, also with a history of high blood pressure but otherwise in excellent health. Shortly after sexual intercourse, his wife found him in a state of confusion wandering around the house. He couldn't remember the events of the previous day. But within twenty-four hours he had recovered and resumed his usual activities, including sexual relations with his wife.

The physician who examined these individuals called the syndrome "transient global amnesia." This syndrome is characterized by an abrupt onset of profound memory loss, without a change in consciousness. The episodes last for several hours, but memory gradually returns to normal. No one really knows the cause of this unusual memory loss, but it seems to be related to hypertension. Fortunately, those who have it experience only a single episode. Therefore, the doctor argued, "one need not discourage patients from resuming their normal sexual activities."

Transient global amnesia is an unusual memory loss since a person who is in the midst of such an attack may show no signs of being different. People have eaten lunch, played golf, driven a car — all while in this amnesic state. But when you ask them for the time or the date, or where they were a few hours earlier, they have forgotten. After a short period of time, the memory may return just as quickly as it was lost, and the person may then go through life without a single further attack.[7]

Drugs and Memory: Alcohol

Drugs such as alcohol, marijuana, and others have distinct effects on memory, although their effects differ according to the subject. The degree to which our memories are impaired depends on the circumstances in which drugs are used, on our own physiological make-up, and on chance.

Cocktail parties are typically gay, boisterous affairs where people become loud and seem to be having a good time. At first glance this may seem a bit surprising, given that alcohol is a depressant, a chemical that slows down neural firing. But alcohol affects the brain, in particular the portions of the brain that seem to specialize in inhibiting social responses of various kinds. When these inhibitory centers are slowed down or turned off, people often say and do things that they ordinarily would not. For example, society places restrictions on certain aggressive and sexual behaviors. Alcohol can release these social inhibitions. Simply put, "The tongue-tied become eloquent, the shy grow bold, the awkward become graceful."[8] It is not surprising, then, that this time-honored drug is mistakenly thought to be a stimulant. Actually, alcohol has a purely depressant effect on the human nervous system, and if it is taken in very large amounts a person becomes completely unconscious.

Alcohol, like most things, affects people in different ways. Depending on a person's mood and the drinking setting, alcohol can have positive or negative effects. Sometimes people become mildly euphoric, sometimes they become a bit withdrawn. For others there are more profound effects. In his book *The Varieties of Religious Experience*, William James put forth his ideas:

> The sway of alcohol over mankind is unquestionably due to its power to stimulate the mystical faculties of human nature, usually crushed to earth by the cold facts and dry criticisms of the sober hour. Sobriety diminishes, discriminates and says no; drunkenness expands, unites, and says yes. It is, in fact, the great exciter of the YES function in man. . . . To the poor and the unlettered it stands in the place of symphony concerts and of literature, and it is part of the deeper mystery and tragedy that whiffs and gleams of something we immediately recognize as excellent, should be vouchsafed to many of us only in the fleeting earlier phases of what, in its totality, is so degrading a poisoning.

Alcohol is absorbed into the bloodstream more or less quickly depending on how full the stomach is, how fast it is drunk, and the strength of the drink. From here it is distributed to every organ in the body and its effects can be felt as soon as it gets to the brain. Two or three ounces of scotch cause a person to feel free of many inhibitions and balance becomes affected. After a few drinks, cognitive processes are notably depressed, as are those functions involved in driving. Wobbly walking and slurring of words are not uncommon. After additional alcohol, the drinker is even more unsteady, and also prone to extreme displays of emotion. Sensory perception becomes affected. Extreme drinking can cause a coma or even death.

After a night of heavy drinking, it is not uncommon to hear a remark such as "I got smashed last night and can't remember a thing." Nor is it uncommon for people to say, "I drink because it helps me to forget." When we flood our bodies with alcohol, is memory really affected? There seems to be very little doubt that regardless of whether a person is an alcoholic, a heavy drinker, or a moderate drinker, the ingestion of a few drinks impairs memory processes. Although most drinkers are unaware that their memory is impaired, laboratory tests demonstrate that alcohol significantly interferes with the efficiency of memory. To find out how alcohol affects memory, investigators have examined whether drinking disrupts the input of new information (storage) or the ability to get access to memory traces (retrieval). The results of several experiments indicate that alcohol interferes with the formation of new memories while leaving retrieval processes relatively intact. It appears that events experienced under the influence of alcohol cannot be as well remembered as events experienced during the sober state.

To examine whether alcohol affects our ability to commit new information to memory, investigators brought seventy-two subjects between twenty-one and thirty-three years old into a laboratory and gave them either a medium dose of alcohol, a high dose of alcohol, or a placebo drink (a drink that tasted just like the others but contained no alcohol). The high dose was equivalent to approximately five or six ounces of 80-proof vodka for a 150-pound person and was mixed with an equal volume of a solution that would mask the taste. The medium dose was about half as much. After drinking, the subjects were shown forty color photographs of outdoor scenes and instructed to pay close attention to the details. They were tested on twenty of the photos. The test was simple: Two photos were shown and the subjects had to say which one had been seen before. One reason for using picture recognition is that it is thought to be a task that minimizes or even eliminates the necessity for a search through long-term memory. If the photo looks sufficiently familiar, the subject simply indicates that it was seen before.

The alcohol had a clear effect on subjects' ability to recognize what they had seen before. The mean number of correct responses was 16.4 for those who had the placebo drink, 15.5 for those who had the medium dose of alcohol, and 14.4 for those who had the high dose. When these results were combined with those of other studies, the investigators were led to conclude, "Our results strongly support the conclusion that the storage phase of memory was impeded by alcohol intoxication." In other words, even when subjects were provided with techniques that should ease retrieval, their memories were still significantly impaired by alcohol.

Next the investigators looked at the effects of alcohol on the retrieval of information previously stored. This was done by giving subjects long word lists to learn while sober. One week later, they were given either a high dose (five to six drinks) of alcohol or a placebo drink. Thus all subjects stored the information while sober and later retrieved that information in either an intoxicated or a sober state. Remarkably enough, the drunk and the sober subjects performed quite similarly on the test of free recall. The mean number of words recalled by the sober people was just about equal to that recalled by those who were intoxicated.

In other words, while alcohol inhibits our ability to process new information, previously learned information can be recalled even in an intoxicated state.

The strongest effects of acute, moderate doses of alcohol are to be found in the storage stage of memory, not in retrieval. Therefore, a loud, boisterous person who is having a great time drinking at a Friday night cocktail party will probably have no difficulty in remembering past events while still at the party, but may have some trouble on Saturday morning remembering conversations and other events of the night before.

It might be of interest to know whether alcohol has any effect on the serial position curve. Recall that when people are given a list of items to remember, the items at the beginning and the end of the list are typically remembered best. Some investigators set out to discover whether this is still the case for people who are recalling under the influence of alcohol.[9]

Subjects in their twenties and early thirties were asked to

get a regular night's sleep before testing and not to drink anything on the evening prior to the test. When they came to the laboratory, they were given either a low dose or a high dose of alcohol — both of which were mixed with an orange drink to mask the flavor. A third group drank a placebo. The low dose was equivalent to three ounces of 95-proof liquor for a 150-pound person, or about two to three mixed drinks. The high dose of alcohol was twice as much, equivalent to about four to six mixed drinks. All subjects were then given a list of twelve words to look at, which had to be recalled immediately after the twelfth word of each list had been presented. The serial position curves are shown here.

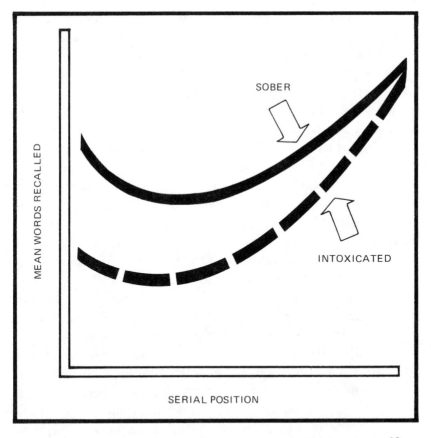

Serial position curves for sober and intoxicated subjects[10]

The results are clear-cut. Alcohol does not produce an overall decrease in recall from all serial positions. Rather, alcohol reduces recall of words from the first part of the list but not from the last part. The last few items, which are dumped from short-term memory, are recalled equally as well by the intoxicated as by the sober. The other items, which come from long-term memory, are not recalled as well. Alcohol seems to leave us able to deal with items in short-term memory, but leads to difficulty in the transfer of information into long-term memory. In other words, people under the influence of alcohol can immediately recall small bits of information, but they have trouble remembering after a period of delay.

When alcohol is absorbed into our body, blood alcohol levels reach a peak and then decline. As a side interest, these investigators looked at whether there was a difference in memory performance depending on whether an individual is heading toward the peak or coming down from it. They found that people perform better on these memory tasks when they are coming down from the peak.

Most of the alcohol studies have been done using men as subjects, but there is some indication that women obtain higher peak blood alcohol levels than males on the same alcohol dose, even when the amount has been adjusted for body weight. There is also some evidence to suggest that women and men absorb and eliminate alcohol at different rates. But does alcohol affect the memory of women differently from that of men? Some investigators decided to try to find out. Using a free recall task, they discovered that alcohol affected females to a greater extent than males. There is some indication then that women do get higher than men.

Another study has been done on the longer-term effects of drinking alcohol.[11] It began with mailing 450 drinking-history questionnaires to a random sample of men living in southern California. From the answers, about one hundred individuals were selected to be studied. Each person was given a number of different tests, some of which were designed to measure overall cognitive ability in general, and others to measure memory recall ability more specifically.

It turns out that there was indeed a relationship between a person's long-term drinking habits and efficiency of cognitive and memory processes. But the relationship was of an unexpected kind. The total amount of pure alcohol a person had drunk over a lifetime did not seem to be related to how well a person did. Nor did it matter how often a person took a drink. What did make a difference was the amount typically consumed on one drinking occasion. The people who regularly drank the most at a single sitting were those who remembered the fewest words on the memory test and performed least well on other tests.

In sum, these investigators found that intellectual performance of social drinkers was negatively associated with the amount of alcohol consumed per drinking occasion. The pattern was strongest in heavy drinkers but was also generally evident in light and moderate drinkers. This seems to suggest, at least as far as memory is concerned, that it would be better to drink one drink every day than to save up until Saturday night and splurge with seven drinks. Even though the same amount of alcohol would be ingested, the effects on the brain are quite different.

The plight of a woman referred to simply as Mrs. S. illustrates the memory problems that can occur in extreme cases of alcoholism. This poor woman was picked up by the police wandering through a city park, wearing a fine mink coat, and talking incoherently to empty air. She was over fifty and obviously wealthy. Saddened by the death of her husband, struggling with unbearable feelings of loneliness, she had begun to drink constantly. Her favorite was gin; she drank it for breakfast, lunch, and dinner, and for in-between snacks. Tragically, the ravages of alcoholism damaged her beyond repair. "She could remember nothing; knew neither who she was nor where she was, what time of year it was, whether it was morning or afternoon."[12]

Mrs. S. had developed a disease called "Korsakoff's

psychosis." While most alcoholics escape its ugly clutches, many suffer all the same from a lesser disturbance in memory. A small percentage of alcoholics will have chronic organic brain damage and serious memory impairment.

A person who has been drinking a fifth of liquor a day for ten years should not be surprised to experience a clouding of memory, sometimes called the alcoholic haze. Happily for alcoholics, these problems largely disappear if and when the person stops drinking. Alcoholics who were tested four to five weeks after starting treatment performed remarkably well on memory tests.[13]

The alcoholic blackout is a story unto itself. *Blackout* is a confusing term that has come to mean memory loss while drinking of events ordinarily remembered. About two-thirds of chronic alcoholics frequently experience memory loss while drinking. But blackouts aren't unique to chronic alcoholics. Surveys of young nonalcoholic men indicate that about one-third have experienced at least one blackout.

No one really knows why some alcoholics never have blackouts while others experience them almost every time they drink. We also do not really understand why some drinkers have blackouts on some occasions but not on other occasions, even though the same amount of alcohol was drunk. There are some situations in which a blackout is more likely to occur:

- When you gulp a large amount very quickly

- When you are extremely tired

- When you've taken sedatives or tranquilizers at the same time as heavy drinking.

Researchers have been able to pinpoint more precisely the memory loss by producing alcoholic blackout in the laboratory. The deficit is very specific. During blackout, assuming the person has not lost consciousness, events from the past can be retrieved from long-term memory, and a person can remember something for a short period of time (short-term memory). But the alcoholic blackout leads to inability to remember an event for any length of time, since the ability to transfer information from short- to long-term memory, where it can be stored for retrieval, is severely impaired.

Two kinds of memory loss are common in blackouts. One is the fragmentary, spotty type where the person only realizes a forgotten event when it is told to him afterward. The other is the *en bloc* memory loss of significant events, which leads to a sense of lost time. The *en bloc* type is usually total and seemingly permanent. No amount of memory jogging, by either oneself or another person, helps the person remember. Having such a blackout can be quite a frightening experience, since often the person wonders whether he or she might have harmed or killed someone else.

As to whether the lost memories can be recovered, it depends on the type of loss. With *en bloc* blackouts, it is very difficult, if not impossible, to recover the memories even when special means such as hypnosis are tried. With fragmentary blackouts, people often have at least partial recovery. However, the returning memory has an unreal quality, "like a picture out of focus," or "like remembering a dream." Alcoholics sometimes complain that they lose their memory while drinking — they forget where they hid the bottle, or where they put their wallet — only to have the memory return when they begin drinking again. This type of situation has sometimes been referred to as "state-dependent learning" — learning that occurs in a particular drug state and cannot be remembered unless the person is drugged again. There is some evidence that this happens with human beings, but the findings have been inconsistent.

Can blackouts be prevented? There is some indication that they are preventable if the drinker is constantly reminded of events that happened a short time after they occur. Providing memory-prompting cues and having the person rehearse what happened "apparently 'grooves in' the memory so that it is recoverable not only thirty minutes after the event occurs but also on the following day *if* cuing is repeated."[14] The person may have difficulty the next day spontaneously remembering an event, but once cued, the memory seems to return. Thus, cuing must take place both immediately after drinking and on the following day in order to minimize memory problems.

Drugs and Memory: Marijuana

The effects of marijuana are similar to those of alcohol — relief of tension, mild euphoria, and subjective feelings of conviviality. It has been used for centuries in some parts of the world, such as India, as both an intoxicant and an aid to medication.

Marijuana has been accused of altering motivation, leading to "harder" drugs, or causing brain damage, but when all is said and done there is really little or no evidence for these charges. But smoking marijuana does have some definite effects. First, it increases the heart rate, even in people who are extremely tolerant of the psychic effects. Second, it causes a reddening of the conjunctiva of the eyes. Finally, it causes a reduction in the flow of saliva — a dry mouth.

To delve into the question of what marijuana exactly does to the mind, a group of psychologists performed the following study: Two groups of volunteer subjects came to a laboratory at a Veterans' Administration hospital in California. The subjects in the "drug" group ate a brownie that contained a colorless resin, THC, the active ingredient in marijuana; those in the "placebo" group also ate a brownie, one that was identical in every respect to the "drug" brownie except that the THC had been removed. There was no way for a particular subject to know whether the brownie just eaten contained the drug or not.

Before eating the brownie, both groups of subjects received ten word lists; after reading each list, they attempted to recall the words. After all ten free recall tests, each subject ate either the drug or the placebo brownie. On hour later, when the marijuana would be having its greatest effect, the subjects were tested on all the words they had seen earlier.

The results of the initial tests are shown on page 98. Since the initial tests were given before the brownies were eaten, we naturally expect no difference between the drug and placebo subjects. The serial position curves were therefore identical (A). Of more interest is the fact that the two groups did not differ in their scores on the test given one hour later (B). This test occurred when the drug subjects were high on marijuana and the placebo subjects were sober. That their performance is identical suggests that marijuana has no effect on the retrieval of information already stored in long-term memory.

Two hours after the brownies had been eaten, when the drug subjects were still high, both groups were again given new word lists and tested after each list. These results look quite different (C). The placebo subjects remembered considerably more than the drug subjects. Since it had already been shown that marijuana does not affect retrieval, the worse performance of the drug group must mean that the drug had the effect of reducing the capacity to store information in long-term memory. The fact that the drug interferes with memory for the beginning and middle items on the list, but not the last few items, is important. Because the last few positions are assumed to reflect recall from short-term memory, the implication of this result is that short-term memory recall is not impaired by marijuana. But as the beginning and middle positions are assumed to reflect recall of items that have been successfully transferred into long-term memory, the poorer recall of items in these positions means that ingesting marijuana affects the transfer from short- to long-term memory.

This conclusion was widely believed for many years. Then, several years ago, a different group of investigators at the University of Kentucky Medical Center began studying recall following marijuana intoxication.[15] As in the earlier

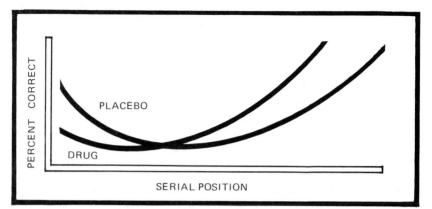

(A) Placebo and drug subjects are identical before eating brownies.

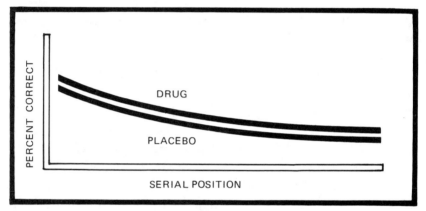

(B) After eating brownies, drug subjects recall "old" information as well as placebo subjects.

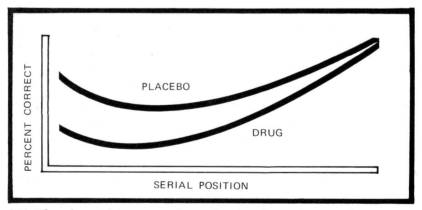

(C) Placebo subjects perform better than drug subjects on free recall task.

work the subjects in their study were randomly assigned to a drug or placebo condition. After hearing and recalling word lists, their serial position curves were obtained. But these did not correspond to those found in the California studies. In this study, *both* the primacy and the recency portions of the curve were reduced by the drug; both short- and long-term memory were adversely affected. The curves looked like those seen here.

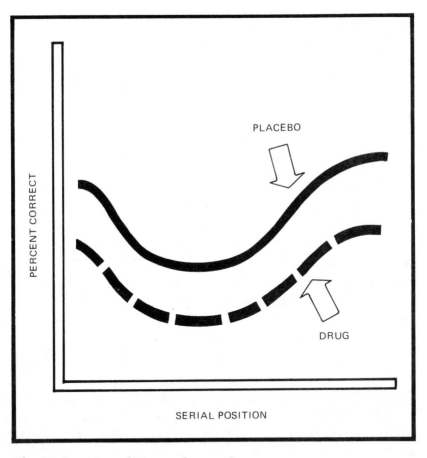

The University of Kentucky study

PAGE 98: *The effects of marijuana on memory*[16]

How can this apparent inconsistency be explained? Quite easily. The California subjects ingested their marijuana in brownies, whereas the Kentucky subjects smoked theirs. When you smoke marijuana rather than eat it, it works faster on the system. Thus, the Kentucky subjects were undoubtedly more stoned than their California counterparts. Taken together, the two sets of studies suggest that low doses of pot (as in the California study) might not disrupt retrieval from short-term memory, whereas higher doses (the Kentucky study) will.

Even though memory storage and possibly retrieval are hurt to some extent by marijuana, the picture is not completely gloomy. It is now believed by some that with sufficient practice, people can learn to perform as well under the influence of marijuana as they do without it.

It is clear that the effect of marijuana will vary enormously depending on the amount of THC it contains. It also depends on how much of the active ingredient is absorbed by the smoker. But many of the effects perceived by smokers may be entirely imaginary. In one study, people were given "marijuana" cigarettes which had all of the resin taken out of them and were therefore no more potent than hay. Could the smokers tell the difference between these cigarettes and others that did contain active marijuana? Not all of them could. Several people claimed that the phony cigarettes were very potent. This suggested to the investigator that we need to study not only the effect of marijuana on the mind, but the effect of the mind on marijuana.[17]

Before we leave the subject of marijuana, we might ask whether there are any long-term effects of smoking on neural functioning while not under the influence. Are there any enduring effects of getting high on grass? The evidence is not all in yet. But even if short-term memory and the capacity to form lasting memories are hurt to some extent by marijuana, it is beginning to look as if, with sufficient practice, people can learn to perform as well having smoked marijuana as they do without it. One person who has considered this question is Rhea Dornbush, a psychologist at New York Medical College. As she points out, scientists have taken two approaches in studying the effects of chronic marijuana use. One has focused on creating populations of regular users by administering marijuana daily for short periods of four to six weeks. The second has focused on existing populations of people who have smoked marijuana for years.

In the typical study of the first sort, subjects smoke marijuana every day for perhaps a month, preceded and followed by nonsmoking periods. When researchers administer the usual word recall tests, they discover that memory performance initially falls off, but then improves. No one is sure why improvement occurs. Apparently some regular users of marijuana can learn to overcome its effects through sheer force of will, by making an effort to think hard and to concentrate so that their attention does not wander.

A word of caution is in order. One of the limiting factors in "created" chronic populations is that the people in them have to agree to be confined in one place for the duration of observation. Not everyone is willing to do that, and the subjects may not be typical marijuana users. Another limitation is that smoking pot once a day for one month, or even for three months, is by no means the same as smoking it for ten or even thirty years.

To follow the second approach, studying existing populations of long-term users, is to face a different set of difficulties. In the United States, it is not easy to find such populations. Therefore data have generally been obtained from users in other countries, often Jamaica or Greece. The findings of a survey in Costa Rica lend at least indirect support to the idea that long-term marijuana users can compensate for any adverse effects on memory.[18] The average subject in the study had smoked about one and a half cigarettes a day for almost seventeen years; many had smoked more than that. In general, the heaviest users had the highest incomes, the least unemployment, and the most stable job histories. The heaviest user of all, who was averaging forty cigarettes a day, was managing a very successful business with eight employees.

One must be cautious in interpreting any study involving experienced marijuana users. These people may have developed strategies for overcoming any cognitive deficits that may accrue under the influence of marijuana. But strictly speaking, the conclusions of the Costa Rican study should not be taken to apply to individuals who are not as experienced in their use of marijuana.

A newspaper reporter doing a story on memory once said that she imagined heaven as the great lost and found department in the sky, a universal drawer containing everything she had ever forgotten, lost, had stolen, or left behind on restaurant chairs or lavatory sinks, in taxicabs and locker rooms. In this drawer, she hoped, would be rings and baubles of various worth, eight sets of car keys, countless notebooks, vitally important papers, and a few obscure objects of desire and lost pride. If heaven were a place where people never went through disasters, never received brain injuries, never took drugs, and didn't age, perhaps it would be a place where memory would function more efficiently. For now, however, we live in a world where these outside influences happen — each day, each week, each year. Researchers are just beginning to understand the consequences for memory.

6
Memory in Older People

On the average, people today are living longer. In this century alone, life expectancy has increased from forty-nine years in 1900 to seventy-three years in 1976, partly due to advances in the prevention and treatment of diseases. This extended life expectancy means many of us will spend more of our lives in the "golden years." It is important then to understand something about how the aging process affects our memories.

As many people know either from bitter personal experience, or from watching a loved one, when people grow old, they often begin to lose their memories. In severe cases, there is a depressing psychological decline in which the events of the day are quickly forgotten. Instead, the person's mind dwells in the distant past. The term *senility* has been used to refer to this condition; it comes from the Latin word meaning "old" or "old man." Simply put, senility is the loss of both physical and mental ability that occurs with advancing age. Unfortunately this condition can place an individual in a

103

highly dependent state in which there is an immense need for outside care.

The typical senile man or woman can usually recall past events or information that has already been stored in long-term memory before senility sets in. However, there is a disruption of ability to store new information. Recent events stay a very short while in short-term memory and then are lost, never making it into long-term memory. Most of the person's references are to the events of the past; these are the only events that have meaning. Thus the present slips away, while memories of the past linger.

Over the years, a number of theories have been advanced in an attempt to explain how and why senility sets in for some people and not others. A fascinating personal recollection, entitled "On Watching Myself Get Old," was recently written by Donald O. Hebb, one of the most influential modern psychologists in the fields of learning and perception, and appeared in *Psychology Today* magazine. His report is an idiosyncratic, inside story of what it has been like for him to grow old. He wrote it at the age of seventy-four.

Hebb noted that the elderly are sometimes considered to be a brain-injured population. The literature shows that although the brain begins to lose weight before the age of thirty, there is no evidence whatsoever for brain cell loss with age. The wild figures tossed around showing that we lose one hundred thousand brain cells a day after the age of thirty (or that every martini kills ten thousand brain cells) simply have no scientific evidence to back them up, Hebb claims, although others disagree. One reason for this is that it is very difficult to obtain tissue from the living brain of healthy people at different ages. Thus, brain experiments tend to be done on other mammals: monkeys, dogs, cats, and rats. These studies have found, according to one respected neuroanatomist, Marian Diamond, that rats do not lose brain cells as they age. She has suggested that we make the optimistic assumption that the same is true of humans rather than the pessimistic assumption of cell loss, for which there is no scientific evidence.

Donald Hebb was aware of the lack of evidence for brain cell loss with age when he wrote his personal account of his own intellectual changes with advancing age. But his approach was that if intellectual activity depends on and is enhanced by a person's experience, why couldn't it improve with advancing age? Hebb derived some support for this notion when he looked at real people, particularly the careers of eminent scientists and writers, some of whom make their greatest contribution in their forties and fifties. Immanuel Kant, for instance, wrote the *Critique of Pure Reason* when he was fifty-seven.

Despite the hope, Hebb noticed some deterioration in certain cognitive abilities. His first realization came when he was forty-seven. He had been reading a scientific article that was directly relevant to his work and as he read, he thought, "I must make a note of this." Then he turned over the page and found a penciled note in his own handwriting. His reaction was one of shock. "I was used to forgetting things that didn't interest me," he said, "but even then I always knew when I was reading something a second time."

Hebb worried after this incident about the possibility of early senility. Then he decided that his memory lapses might just be due to the fact that he was doing too much — research, teaching, writing, directing a new laboratory, chairing an academic department. He slowed down a bit, quit working in the evenings, began taking a full hour for lunch, started reading less instead of trying to read everything. The result was that his memory for what he read soon came back to its "normal, haphazard effectiveness."

The losses that gerontologists usually talk about started for Hebb in his sixties. His sensory acuity was diminished a bit, his balance, walking, and rising from a sitting position became somewhat less steady, and his forgetfulness increased. But in addition to these, he felt that his effective vocabulary was declining, his thought patterns were repeating themselves, and his motivation was grossly changed. Hebb took these to indicate a "slow, inevitable loss of cognitive capacity." This conclusion seems odd from a man who, at age seventy-four, is still an honorary professor at a Canadian university and an avid fan of the tough crossword puzzles in the London *Observer.* One editor at the magazine that published his recollection was prompted to observe: "If Dr. Hebb's faculties continue to deteriorate in the manner he suggests, by the end of the next decade he may be only twice as lucid and eloquent as the rest of us."

Other noted social scientists have similarly speculated on the cognitive changes that might occur with advancing age. The last ten years or so have seen a growing interest in experimental studies of adult age differences in human memory. Instead of asking the general question "Does memory get worse as we age?" these studies have looked at very specific memory processes or stages and attempted to determine whether any age differences exist.

The leading experts in the field of aging are now convinced that even though performance in some kinds of memory situations may weaken a bit with age, other cognitive skills are fully maintained with advancing age. Furthermore, even though performance may weaken, it is only "average" performance — the performance of the "average" older person when compared to the performance of the "average" younger person. But there are great individual differences among people. One person may show some decline with advancing age while another shows no decline.[1] As far as memory is concerned, people do not have to grow old. In light of this, investigators in this area have begun to dispel the myth of an overall decline with advancing age. This should be kept in mind when reading about any "average" drop-off in ability to remember various kinds of materials. However, we can still ask whether there are any changes with age in the functioning of sensory memory, short-term memory, or long-term memory. Psychologists now know a great deal about this question.[2]

Sensory Memory and Aging

Recall from Chapter 2 that the three-stage model of memory involves transfers from sensory to short-term to long-term memory. In his studies of sensory memory, George Sperling briefly showed arrays of digits or letters to people. After a short while, a cue was presented that told people which row in the array they should report. When the cue was delayed for a second or so, the ability to reproduce the information that had been seen deteriorated. This decline is thought to be caused by the rapid decay of a visual trace.

To discern whether or not there are age differences in sensory memory, investigators have tested subjects of different ages on a version of the Sperling task. Typically, older people fare as well as younger ones, suggesting that any cognitive difficulties that elderly people have do not lie in sensory memory processing, at least not as far as vision is concerned.[3]

But there may be a bit of a problem for older people when it comes to material that is presented not to the eyes but to the ears. The cocktail party phenomenon is one in which a person is in the middle of a crowded, noisy group, with one conversation going on to the right and another just to the left. Since both conversations impinge on the sense organ, both enter sensory memory. But as people can pay attention to only one conversation at a time, only one at a time can be transferred into short-term memory.

Psychologists have done experiments to study what happens when two streams of information simultaneously impinge on the ears. The experiments are not done at an actual cocktail party, where it is hard to control all that is happening, but instead in a laboratory using what is called a dichotic listening task. The subject wears earphones connected to a stereo tape recorder. One message is played through the left earphone and at the same time a completely different message is played through the other earphone. The subject is asked to pay attention to one of the messages. To make sure that this is done, the subject is asked to "shadow" the attended message, or to repeat it back aloud as it is being played.

In the typical dichotic listening experiment, subjects do not remember much of what is played to the unattended ear. Occasionally, a person remembers if his or her own name is played, but very little else. If subjects are suddenly and unexpectedly stopped in the midst of shadowing and asked to recall what they can from the unattended message, they are often able to report back only the last few things that had been presented. Taken together, the results of these experiments indicate attended information is transferred to short-term memory, while unattended information decays rapidly and is therefore not remembered.

In cases in which just a few items, such as numbers or letters, are presented simultaneously to each ear, subjects do a bit better. If the items are presented quickly, the subjects will typically first recall all items from one ear before recalling items from the other. It is thought that while the items from the attended ear are being reported, the ones from the unattended ear are held briefly in an auditory sensory memory where they are subject to rapid decay unless they are quickly recalled.

With these procedures in mind, some psychologists have carried out studies to explore the effects of aging on dichotic listening performance.[4] Using subjects that ranged in age from twenty to sixty, the investigators found that older people are just as good as younger ones at recalling the items in the attended ear, but when they attempted to recall the items from the unattended ear, they performed more poorly. Their results are shown in the graph opposite. Note that the first-ear performance shows no age decrement since these items are not held very long in sensory memory. The second-ear items must be held in sensory memory, and performance on these shows a more rapid loss with increasing age. This same pattern of results has been found when the presented material consists of words rather than numbers or letters, although a few studies have shown some loss in first-ear performance as well. Taken together, the results show that these short-term deficits in the elderly cannot all be due completely to loss of motivation, since the older subjects are as accurate as their younger counterparts in remembering the items presented to the first ear. It is also not the case that older people simply choose to attend to one ear only, because similar results were observed when the ear to be recalled first was specified after the material had been presented.

There have been many theories advanced to explain the age-related decrements in the dichotic listening situation. One has been suggested; namely, that the second ear's items must be held for a short while in an auditory sensory memory and that material here is lost more rapidly with age. A second theory is that older people are more vulnerable to interfer-

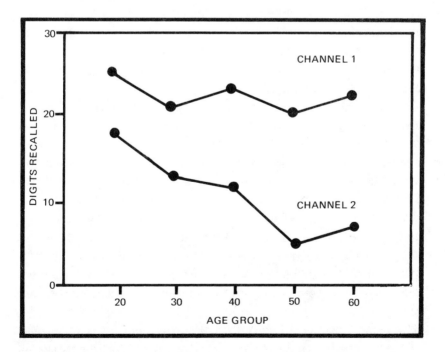

Recall of digits and aging (From Inglis and Caird, 1963)

ence, in this case from the items that have been presented to the first ear. A third possibility is that older people are simply poor at dividing their attention. When they must expend energy deciding how to divide attention, there is less capacity for actually perceiving what is presented. If the processing capacity of the elderly is differentially reduced in this way, they would process information less deeply and poorer retention would result.[5]

Short-term Memory and Aging

A general conclusion is that age differences in short-term memory functioning are negligible.[6] Let us examine some of the evidence behind this.

Earlier, the classic serial position effect was described. To reiterate briefly, when people have to remember a list of items, the first few items and the last few items have the best chance of being remembered. The items at the end of the list are remembered well (the recency effect) because they are typically in short-term memory at the moment the list is recalled. The contents of short-term memory can be "dumped out," after which long-term memory can be searched for additional items. Several investigators have demonstrated that older people show as much recency as do younger people, indicating that short-term memory is unimpaired by aging.

A memory span procedure is also a way of measuring short-term memory capacity. Such a procedure is very simple and often used in IQ testing. A subject is read a string of items (for example, a string of numbers such as 7824956) and is then required to repeat as many of them as possible. The experiment begins with a rather small number of items in the string, such as two or three, which is relatively easy for most people. Then the string is increased until the subject begins to make errors in recollection. The capacity of short-term memory has been defined as the maximum number of items the subject can repeat back perfectly. On the average, people can repeat seven digits and five words without too much trouble.

When testing subjects of different ages, some investigators have found no significant age differentiation in the number of items that can be repeated, while others have found slight age decrements. In one study, people were presented letters and had to repeat them back. The results show that twenty-year-old subjects repeat an average of 6.7 letters while seventy-year-olds could repeat an average of 5.4, a somewhat substantial distinction.

One problem with interpreting these results as showing an age-related decrement in memory span is that the ability to repeat back a string of items depends not only on short-term memory, but also on long-term memory. A few of the items presented move into long-term memory only to be retrieved when the string is reproduced. Thus, the slight age decrements in the memory span can be caused by a decrement in a long-term memory component. The conclusion reached by the experts here, then, is that the performance of older people on short-term memory tasks is not impaired, unless, of course, those tasks involve the division of attention.

How long does it take for information to be forgotten from short-term memory? As we saw in Chapter 2, very little is available after about twenty seconds. Experiments on forgetting from short-term memory have been conducted with subjects of different ages. A typical result is that the rates of memory loss are identical for all age groups, a finding observed by many investigators.

In conclusion, then, short-term retention situations usually involve retrieval of information from short-term memory. However, occasionally short-term retention will reflect some retrieval from long-term memory. Age differences in short-term memory functioning alone are at most minimal if we assume that the item to be reported has been fully perceived in the first place. When a short-term retention task involves long-term memory, then there may be some decrement.

Long-term Memory and Aging

In long-term memory functioning, age differences are often observed. Since long-term memory plays an important role in mental life, this means that elderly people will perform more poorly than their younger counterparts on a variety of mental tasks.

When people are presented with a list of items to remember, they customarily forget the items in the middle. Older people perform as well as younger ones on the last few items; that is, they show an identical recency effect. Older subjects, however, recall fewer items from the beginning and middle of the lists. Since recall from the beginning and middle of the list is from long-term memory, these results indicate that the elderly are somewhat poorer at recalling information from their long-term store.

Later investigations have shown that older people are helped a great deal when provided with good retrieval cues. If we provided the information that one of the items on the list is a fruit or an animal, the elderly person is helped enormously. Taken together, the collection of studies leads to some tentative conclusions about the effect of age on long-term memory functioning. First, the elderly person is at greatest disadvantage when little or no retrieval information is provided and must rely on innate abilities to generate retrieval cues. It may be that the elderly are intellectually less flexible and creative in this self-generation; thus, their memory performance suffers. It seems we are blaming memory problems of the elderly on problems with retrieving information from long-term memory. However, it also appears that the elderly have problems with the initial information storage in long-term memory. Older people seem to fail to organize material as effectively as younger people, and this failure leads to poorer recall later on. This conclusion comes from studies in which people were given instructions to help them organize material more efficiently. Such instructions were most beneficial to older people. In other words, when people are aided in organization, age differences in memory performance are drastically reduced.

Until now, memory experiments have involved lists of items not particularly meaningful to people. For example, the ability to reproduce or recognize geometric designs is often used, an ability that seems to drop off with age. The loss, however, is not very great until the age of sixty or seventy. In another study, young and old subjects learned a series of twenty line drawings. After about a month, the young subjects recognized an average of nineteen of the drawings, while the old ones recognized about sixteen. It makes intuitive sense that older people might be less penalized when the information to be remembered is meaningful to them. Unfortunately, even with more meaningful material, the older subject still shows some deficit.

In one study, men between the ages of twenty-three and seventy-nine were shown scenes recorded on silent film.[7] One scene showed a four-second shot of a young boy inflating a bicycle tire. Another showed a man winding up a watch, while still another showed a car crossing a bridge. To conceal the purpose of the experiment, the subjects were told to try to read the lips of a commentator after each scene was presented. This also ensured that they would pay attention to each of the scenes. Then, much to their surprise, the men were asked to remember the information in the scenes. The results are shown here.

	Age (years)				
	20s	30s	40s	50s	60s +
High	54	57	57	52	32
Low	46	48	48	44	34

Recall of visual scenes (From Farrimond, 1968)

For men of both high and low intelligence, recall declined with advancing age. Recall appears to be at its best with subjects in their mid-forties. Serious decline is not noticeable with subjects under sixty years of age.

Very Long-term Memory

One of the widely accepted myths is that older people are not able to remember events that happened to them recently, whereas memory for things that happened long ago is fine. This may be the case for individuals who are senile, but what about ordinary folks? The evidence for this belief is entirely anecdotal and is usually based upon the recollection of a few important incidents from earlier in life. The problem with using these anecdotes to support the belief in poor recent memory but good long-ago memory is that many of our childhood and young adult experiences have been recalled many times since they happened. An older person who appears to have a vivid memory of college graduation, for example, has inevitably recalled that event many times. The memory then is not from fifty years ago, but partially from the time the event was last recalled.

One study conducted in the 1940s tested new and old memories with subjects of all ages.[8] To test old memories, subjects were asked to recall such things as their age, where they were born, the name of the President, and the names of objects. As a test of new memories, the subjects were asked to recall digits, sentences, and the details of a story that they had just read. Some of the results, as illustrated opposite, show that recall of both kinds of memories declined with age, with the age decrement for new memories being much greater. There is, however, a serious problem in interpreting these results; namely, that the "old" items were completely different from the "new" items. Where a person is born is not comparable to what one read recently in a story. What is needed is a study in which the old and new memories are for comparable items.

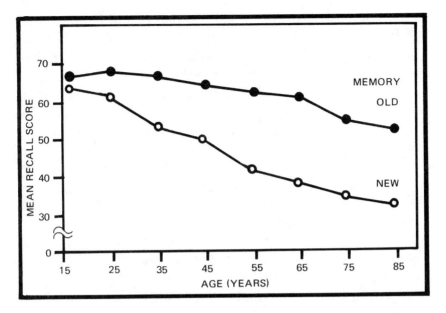

Recall of old and newly learned material as a function of age (From Shakow, Dolkart, and Goldman, 1941, and Botwinick, 1978)

In the last ten years, different investigators have considered the question of remote memories. In these more recent experiments, comparable memory items were used. Even though the memories of older people in these studies were surprisingly good, their results were poorer than those of their younger counterparts in recalling and recognizing events from the remote past. In one case, people were asked to remember news items from one month to two years previously.[9] As expected, the longer it had been since a news item occurred, the poorer the recollection of it. However, it was also found that older adults (over fifty-five) did not perform as well as those under forty. This also occurred when the subjects had to recognize well-known faces; performance declined with increasing age.

When asked to remember the names and faces of their high school classmates, the elderly again perform reasonably well, but less well than the young.[10] Almost four hundred high school graduates who ranged in age from seventeen to seventy-four were tested with names and pictures from their past. The subjects were divided into nine groups based upon the amount of time since high school graduation. The first group had finished school a few months prior to the experiment; the ninth group had been out of school at least forty years. All were tested on their memories of faces and names of their high school classmates in a series of six tests. While each test shows a drop-off in performance with advancing age, it should be noted that people of all ages generally remember quite well. In the words of the investigators, "We were unprepared for our subjects' impressive ability to recognize the names and faces of their old classmates. Those who had recently graduated from high school could correctly identify nine out of ten of their classmates' pictures, but so could people who had graduated thirty-five years earlier, and it made no difference whether they graduated from small or very large classes." Even the subjects who left high school more than forty years before, who were in their late fifties and early sixties, could identify three-fourths of their classmates.

Many people suffer memory impairments in later life. Unfortunately, very little work has been aimed at minimizing such memory problems. Instead, there has been a concentration on work directed at understanding exactly why these problems occur. The evidence seems to indicate that sensory memory functioning does not change with age, and short-term memory functioning declines only slightly, if at all. The real problems are in storing and retrieving new information, which are functions of long-term memory. While children sometimes fail to benefit from training, the elderly often show marked improvement with instructions that help them store more efficiently or from the provision of cues that help them retrieve.

Older people can help themselves avoid a number of memory problems by organizing life events for more efficient storage. Also, it is possible to seek retrieval cues that can help release information from long-term memory. For example, if a person has gone to the grocery store but forgotten the shopping list, there are several ways in which the list can be remembered. One is to generate categories of items: Did I need any meats? any vegetables? any canned goods? These categories serve as excellent retrieval cues.

This is just the beginning, however. Ongoing research by social scientists is trying to develop new strategies and techniques for helping to cope with the memory problems of older people.

An Upbeat Final Note

The studies on memory and aging generally use what is called a cross-sectional method. That is, different groups of people are studied at one point in time; some of them may be young, some middle-aged, and some elderly. More difficult to use is the longitudinal method, in which the same people are followed through different age levels: The same people are observed when they are young, middle-aged, and elderly.

The problem with cross-sectional studies is that they provide only group averages. They cannot tell you anything about how a particular individual will change over a lifetime. A cross-sectional study sometimes produces findings that contradict those obtained when the same individual is observed at different times in life. The classic example is the development of intelligence during the life of an adult. Cross-sectional studies that look at different groups of people at the same time have indicated an early decline beginning at about the age of thirty. But longitudinal studies that consider the same individuals at different points in time have shown no change in intellectual performance — and sometimes an increase — until age fifty or even sixty.[11]

One reason for this discrepancy is the cohort effect. People born in 1890 are part of the same cohort; they have the same biocultural history. Similarly, people born in 1900 are part of a different cohort. In one study, the intellectual performance of people of different ages was examined in both 1956 and again in 1963.

If we looked only at cross-sectional data (different people tested at one point in time), we would see a decline in performance with increasing age. Thus, in 1956, the seventy-year-olds as a group performed worse than the forty-five-year-olds. However, the longitudinal data (same people tested twice) show that there is not a decline, but an increase in intelligence with increasing age. Every cohort showed this effect, with one of the largest increases being for the seventy-year-olds who were tested in 1956. They were better off at the age of seventy-seven than at seventy.

It is important to note that people the same age in 1963 outperformed those who were the same age in 1956. For example, the fifty-nine-year-olds tested in 1963 outperformed the fifty-nine-year-olds tested in 1956. One explanation for this is the general societal improvements at the time the 1904-born people were in school. A better environment and better schools could mean that the 1904 cohort had more intellectual stimulation while growing up than the 1897 cohort.

Cohort effects should be kept in mind when evaluating the declines that are observed in cross-sectional studies on the effects of aging on memory. The seventy-year-olds as a group may be poorer in recognizing the faces of their high school friends than the forty-year-olds as a group. But chances are that when the same individuals are tested at different periods in time, many will not show this decline in ability with age.

7 The Consequences of Imperfect Memory

When people write about their lives, they generally rely heavily on memory. As readers, we rarely find reason to doubt their recollections. "The Guilt of Sons, the Lies of Fathers" is a memoir of a father's extraordinary love and deception. It illustrates some basic thing that happens when we think back over our own lives. The author remembers:

> I was born in Hollywood in 1937. Was a baby in Redondo Beach and a little squirt in Palos Verdes. Drove east at four in a twelve-cylinder Packard convertible to New York. Father went to England to work with the Royal Air Force. I heard the radio tell about Pearl Harbor — my second or third memory — at the Elm Tree Inn, Farmington, Connecticut.[1]

Our very earliest memories usually date back to the age of four or five. The reason that we cannot remember further back has to do with the fact that without language, we do not

119

seem to have the skills for categorizing our experiences and storing them in a way they can be remembered.

> One night in New York, I was in the bedroom I shared with my younger brother, Toby, who was crying; my mother and father were quarreling about money in the kitchen, next door. I was playing with blocks, and my tower fell against the kitchen door. My father came boiling through the doorway in fury; he thought I had been eavesdropping. He hit me across the ear with his open hand, and I was rigid with fear and confusion and couldn't even stammer. . . . He hit my head and arms and legs, never with his fists, shouting from incomprehensible frustration, and finally I found the words to beg him to stop.

Despite the vividness with which someone tells about an experience from the past, we must always keep in mind that the recollection may be very different from the actual experience. Perhaps the father really hit his son across the ear. Perhaps not. People can come to believe they saw and heard things that never really happened. This can be seen so crisply in the reminiscences of psychologist Jean Piaget:

> There is also the question of memories which depend on other people. For instance, one of my first memories would date, if it were true, from my second year. I can still see, most clearly, the following scene, in which I believed until I was about fifteen. I was sitting in my pram, which my nurse was pushing in the Champs Elysées, when a man tried to kidnap me. I was held in by the strap fastened round me while my nurse bravely tried to stand between me and the thief. She received various scratches, and I can still see vaguely those on her face. Then a crowd gathered, a policeman with a short cloak and a white baton came up, and the man took to his heels. I can still see the whole scene, and can even place it near the tube station. When I was about fifteen, my

parents received a letter from my former nurse saying that she had been converted to the Salvation Army. She wanted to confess her past faults, and in particular to return the watch she had been given as a reward on this occasion. She had made up the whole story, faking the scratches. I, therefore, must have heard, as a child, the account of this story, which my parents believed, and projected into the past in the form of a visual memory.[2]

Autobiographical anecdotes from well-known people are interesting in their own right and are occasionally suggestive of techniques and strategies people have for remembering their own life's experiences. Why is it important to understand how we remember the past? Our memories of the past affect our appreciation of where future actions will lead, and thus an understanding of what actions will lead to happy outcomes, and what will lead to tragedy. We calibrate our future upon our past. To paraphrase a number of different scholars of memory, "Those who don't remember the past are doomed to repeat it." Thus, the accuracy of our memories is the basis for our own self-improvement. Understanding *how* we remember the past will help us avoid deception and live a more truthful life. We can gain some insights from social scientists, who fortunately have had a keen interest in understanding how people remember the past.

Remembering Details

"What do you mean, you don't remember? That was the party where John made such a fool of himself; he actually tried to eat the artificial ivy."

"Was that the same party where he tried to put the poodle in the punch bowl?"

"No. No. Not that one. That was years ago. You mean you really don't remember?"

A fascinating article on remembering by a University of Utah psychologist, Marigold Linton, begins with these "memories." Linton had always been interested in studying people's ability to remember events that had occurred in their lives. When she began this work, her first question was "Where can I find some people who will be available for a long period of time, who are reliable, who won't move away, who won't get bored with the study, and whom I could conveniently follow on a regular basis?" The only person she could find who satisfied all of these criteria was herself. She would be the sole subject.

Every day for the six-year period from 1972 until 1977, she wrote down what happened to her. Each memory was recorded on a separate card in the form of a brief description, such as "I have dinner at the Canton Kitchen; delicious lobster dish," or "I land at Orly Airport in Paris." On the back of each card she wrote the date for each event, and then gave it a rating in terms of how important, emotional, or surprising the event was. By 1977 she had written down descriptions of more than five thousand items.

Every month she tested her memory. She picked about 150 cards at random from the file and read the descriptions. Each item could be anywhere from one day to six years old, and for each she tried to remember as quickly as possible when the event had occurred. Linton reasoned that the more information she had about an event and its context, the more accurately it could be dated. Each month she spent from eight to twelve hours testing her memory in this way.

Linton learned some interesting things about her own memory. After about six months of studying herself, she found she would typically be quite depressed after each test session. The reason was that her general procedure was to "warm up" before each test by simply thinking over the highlights of her life over the previous year. During these warm-up exercises, she usually thought of happy times — friends, successes, a good life. But when she started pulling the individual events from her file box, she discovered that the cards contained not only happy memories but also numerous irritations: Her car breaks down and she can't find anyone to help; she fights with a lover; she gets a paper rejected by a scientific journal. Once she realized the source of stress, it seemed to help reduce it.

After six years of studying her memory, she transferred all the information to special computer cards and fed them to a computer. The computer analyses revealed that by the end of any one year, she had forgotten 1 percent of the items written during that year. By the time those items were about two years old, she had forgotten about 5 percent more. Forgetting continued so that by the time the study ended, she had forgotten over 400 items of the 1,350 she wrote down for 1972, or about 30 percent. In general she seemed to forget things at a low, fairly steady rate, with the numbers of forgotten items usually increasing slightly from year to year.

What kinds of things did she remember? Most of the memories were fairly unique, nonrepeated events, like a traffic accident, or surprising events, like a tennis game in which one of the players was injured. It was pretty easy to supply a date for "the tennis game in which Ed got hit in the eye." However, she could not remember the names of the other players in the game. Assuming that Linton's memory processes are like most of ours, this suggests that people remember general information for some time, but that many details drop out.

Overall, Linton's results suggest that specific memories are regularly dropping out. They are not locked in memory for all time, unless they are repeated or relived or unless they are unusually significant. Despite these apparent losses, all is not gloomy. After several phone calls from the same person, it may not be possible to remember any one conversation or even when it took place. But it becomes easier and easier to identify and remember the person's voice. This means that even though specific events are forgotten, considerable knowledge is retained. The mind, Linton thought, undergoes a spring cleaning.

Remembering Events

One of the ways that we remember our past experiences is through the use of landmarks. These are particular events in our lives that are especially important to us, a birthday, graduation from high school, our wedding day. By using these landmark days we can recollect a great deal about our past lives. To show this, psychologist Donald Norman asked people such questions as "What were you doing sixteen months ago?" or "What were you doing on Monday afternoon in the third week of September two years ago?" Most people have an initial reaction along the lines of "You've got to be kidding," but then they make a serious attempt to remember:

SUBJECT: "Come on. How should I know?"

EXPERIMENTER: "Just try it, anyhow."

SUBJECT: "OK, let's see: Two years ago . . . I would be in high school in Pittsburgh. . . . That would be my senior year. Third week in September — that's just after summer — that would be in the fall term. . . . Let me see. I think I had chemistry lab on Mondays. I don't know. I was probably in the chemistry lab. . . . Wait a minute — that would be the second week of school. I remember he started off with the atomic table — a big, fancy chart. I thought he was crazy, trying to make us memorize that thing. You know, I think I can remember sitting. . . ."[3]

This attempt to remember something that happened two years before illustrates how we accomplish recollections of this sort. First we try to rephrase the question in the form of a specific date and then try to determine what we were doing around that time ("that's just after summer — that would be the fall term . . ."). We search memory using prominent features, or landmarks from our past. These landmarks are used as starting points in our search through memory ("my senior year"). Remembering something that happened a couple of years ago is not an easy thing to do. Typically people remember fragments of what they experienced ("a big fancy chart") with reconstructions and inferences of what must have actually happened ("I think I can remember sitting . . .").

Another example of the use of landmarks is in answer to a question such as this one: "At what time did you first leave home five days ago?" College students who were asked this question typically first remembered the time of their first class of the day, and then some event that occurred just before they left home. They moved from that prior event to the time that they left home for school. A person's first class of the day is generally a salient event, since getting to class on time is important to most people. Because of this it is something of a landmark.

One serious problem with studies in which people are asked questions about their past is that it is nearly impossible to distinguish between what is actually remembered and what is reconstructed. Adding a fringe of untruth probably happens to nearly all of our everyday reports of events, whether those events happened recently or long ago. Once this occurs, the new version then becomes the memory. Because the new version seems so real, it is practically impossible to distinguish it from a true memory.

The memories of circumstances in which very surprising and/or consequential events are learned have been termed "flashbulb memories" by psychologists.[4] Hearing the news that President Kennedy had been shot is the prototypical case. The Kennedy assassination created an extraordinarily powerful and widely shared flashbulb memory.

In 1973, ten years after the assassination, *Esquire* magazine asked some famous people where they were when they first heard the news. Julia Child was in the kitchen eating *soupe de poisson*. Billy Graham was on the golf course. Julian Bond was in a restaurant. Tony Randall was in the bathtub. These crisp memories led the author of the *Esquire* article to subtitle it: "Nobody forgets."

The Kennedy assassination is not the only event that has created flashbulb memories for people. Other assassinations, highly newsworthy events, and personally significant events can leave one with a flashbulb memory. The main ingredient seems to be a very high level of surprise, often accompanied by emotional arousal. The name *flashbulb memory* is a reasonably good name for the phenomenon since it suggests surprise and brevity. But the name is not perfect. A photograph taken by flashbulb preserves everything within its scope. Flashbulb memories do not.

The notion that these events should cause a "permanent registration" in the brain is one for which there is no evidence. No one verified that Julia Child was really in the kitchen eating *soupe de poisson*. And, even if she had been, is she remembering the actual experience, pulling out the intact original memory, or is she simply remembering one of the many times she told the tale to another person? Usually the psychologist who is studying flashbulb memories is not in a position to verify the memory. But occasionally one is lucky. One psychologist serendipitously discovered an error. She asked people, "What were you doing when John Kennedy was assassinated?" and got this answer from someone whom she had known quite well at the time of the assassination:

> When I'm reminded of that date, particularly by you, I remember that you were the one who told me about the assassination, or at least that's the way I remember it. . . . I believe that you, I know that you came down and told me about what you . . . had heard on the news. I don't know what time it was. Because down in the hole in ——— Hall one tended to lose track of time. . . . I had been working for some extended period of time and I was very much concentrating on what I was doing when I was interrupted by you having heard something about it. You said, I'm sure it was you who said, "The President has been assassinated, or shot — shot." And I probably looked up and said, "What?" and you said, "Kennedy, he's been shot." And I said, "What do you mean? Where?" and you said you didn't know. . . .[5]

The problem with flashbulb memories was dramatically revealed: The psychologist was nowhere near her respondent at the time of the assassination. Could she have been wrong? Examination of documentable external events demonstrated that the two people could not have been at the same place at the time Kennedy was killed. This means that the events described by this individual, although provided with great detail, emotion, and conviction, could not and did not happen.

One of the determinants of flashbulb memories might be rehearsal. To discover whether this was so, each subject in a study was asked — if he or she gave a flashbulb account of an incident at all — how often it had been related to someone else:

"Never told anyone."

"Gave the same account roughly one to five times."

"Gave the same account roughly six to ten times."

"Gave the same account more than ten times."

Just as suspected, the subjects reported that they had related their personal tales more than once and generally between one and ten times. Thus it appears as if frequent rehearsals of these events may account in part for why they occur.

The other important ingredient seems to be high importance. The investigators suggested that when something important happens and attention is sustained at a high level for some time, a flashbulb memory is potentially created.

How interesting an experience is also determines how likely we are to remember it. What makes something interesting? Suppose a friend told you, "I was walking down the street when suddenly. . . .

a) I saw a cat.
b) I decided to tie my shoe.
c) I decided to eat some chalk.

d) I heard a loud noise.
e) I heard an incredible boom.
f) I heard a cricket.
g) I saw a dead child."

Some of these things are more interesting than others. For example, seeing a cat, deciding to tie his shoe, and hearing a cricket are totally uninteresting. They seem strange in the sentence because the word *suddenly* leads you to expect something a bit more interesting. Deciding to eat some chalk is pretty interesting, and so is hearing a loud noise, particularly one that is so loud as to be characterized as an "incredible boom." Seeing a dead child, however gory and unpleasant, is highly interesting. From these examples, we can reach some conclusions about the degree of interest. Unusual happenings are more interesting than usual ones and noises are interesting, particularly very loud noises. Death is also interesting.

People worry about death, for themselves and for loved ones. This is one reason why it is interesting. But death is not interesting in every instance. If you hear that Mrs. Jones died yesterday and you have no idea who Mrs. Jones is, the fact that she died will not be very interesting. If, on the other hand, you hear that Mrs. Jones died while piloting a Cessna 152 aircraft and you happen to own one, even if you don't know Mrs. Jones, you might find her death interesting. Obviously, then, only some deaths are interesting. People are much more interested in reading the front page of a newspaper or the sports section than they are in reading the obituaries. This is, in part, due to the fact that death is interesting when it is unexpected, and unexpected events are interesting.

Other interesting things, according to Yale computer scientist Roger Schank, are danger, power, sex, money (in large quantities), destruction, chaos, romance, disease, and many other concepts of this type.

What we remember from our past depends upon many factors, but the most obvious of them is interest. As we go through life, we experience a continuous stream of input from our environment, from which we pick out what we find interesting. These are the things we tell to others, and the things we tend to remember ourselves. Much of our world is barely noticed until there is some reason to pay attention. To uninteresting events we do not pay attention; we do not bother to try to understand or explain these events. To interesting events we pay attention.

Shifting Landmarks

When we stop to mull over some part of our past, we remember especially unusual landmark events that stand out from day-to-day experiences. But these events are not representative parts of our life. Our wedding day, the day father died, the day JFK was assassinated — these are the pegs on which memory hangs together. They are not randomly chosen days; indeed they are very special.

As we reconstruct a landmark event, our mental image suffers first from the attrition of details, but also from subsequent manipulation. We overemphasize them and underemphasize everything else. Landmarks tend to be shared memories: We shared the wedding with spouse and family, we shared our father's death with siblings and other relatives. We recall these events repeatedly, in conversations with others or while alone, and each time we do this we are likely to give a slightly different interpretation to the event. We replace one memory with a slightly altered one.

It is easy to find examples of mental landmarks that have shifted in meaning. Two people remembered their wedding quite fondly a year after it happened, but ten years later, after a bitter divorce, the wedding was remembered as a hectic, frightening, unpleasant experience. The shifting of landmark memories is a part of life.

Remembering People

Suppose you were asked to remember the people with whom you went to high school. In one study people were tested for their ability to remember events both a few years old and twenty years old. The participants were asked to remember the names of their classmates; they worked on this task for days, and in some cases, months. The longer they tried to remember, the more names they came up with. The graph opposite shows one person's progress at remembering her classmates.

As the participants in this study tried to remember names, they were directed to think out loud. Here is what one individual said (the names are changed to protect privacy):

Subject: I was trying to think of Carl's last name but I just can't think of it. Umm, okay, let me see if there's any other neighborhoods that I haven't gotten to that I can remember where people my age lived. Um . . . humm. There is no one that lived way up on the end . . . And now I'm trying to think of the Sunset Cliffs down on Cal Western 'cause a lot of people always used to go there and go tide pool picking and just run around and go surfing. I'm trying to think of all the people that perhaps went surfing or even tide pool picking that were in my grade. Um . . . if I could see them lined up against — there's this one cliff down at Newbreak Beach they always used to line up with their boards and sit down and look at the waves, and then I go down the row and see if there's anybody I haven't already named. There's Benny Nesbit, I already named him, and Dave Culbert and they used to go surfing, and um there are a lot of older people too. Um, Joe Nate, I already named them, all those guys used to go surfing. Um, he was older — he was older — and older — he was younger. A lot of those guys were older. Let me see, him and him . . . Okay I was just going down the list and I don't see anybody that I haven't already seen and there was this one girl who always used to be down there, but she was younger. I already named the people that she hangs around with. Um, is there anybody else that I know that used to . . .

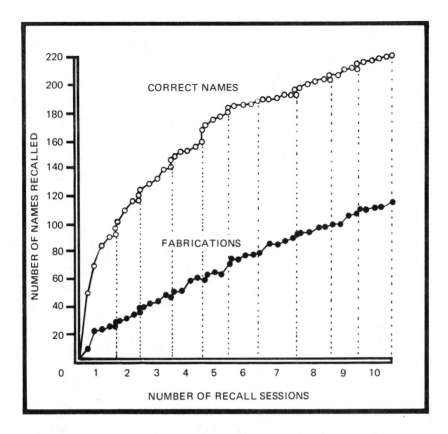

Remembering classmates from school (From Williams, 1976, and Lindsay and Norman, 2nd ed., 1977)

Several things are obvious from this. First, when a participant reports aloud the things he or she thinks he was doing, it is possible to discover something about the strategies that are used. In this case, it appears as if retrieving names involved a process of reconstruction. The entire setting was first retrieved, and then the names. A considerable amount of time was spent re-creating the actual setting where the experiences took place. Then the subject was able to list the people whom he imagined in the setting.

One interesting thing that people did in this study was to "overshoot." They continued to remember new information about a person long after their actual name had been found in memory. What purpose does overshoot serve? It helps to provide information that can be used to confirm that the person whose name was recalled was actually one of the people being searched for. This additional information provides a check on the validity of the name. A second purpose is to provide more content, to generate new settings from which new names can be plucked. Here is an example of actual recall which shows the subject shifting from one context to another, picking up pockets of people at each stop (names have again been changed):

Subject: Umm I was picturing the people that I knew, and trying to see if there was anyone missing. I'm pic — picturing a familiar place and I just located two more. There's Mike Peterhill and um (tapping) Larry Atkinson. I located them at their house, or at Larry's house where they work on cars.

Experimenter: Mm-hm.

Subject: OK? And that was next door to Arlene and next door to Bill, um OK, and then oh um, there was my old girlfriend (laugh). I wonder why I remembered her. Um, I remembered her because I remembered the, I was thinking about the house where Larry lives, and was remem — remembering going to visit him once while he was working on this old, uh car, Pack, old Packard and Mary was there, so that's her, and then her friends now are Jane and, uh . . . What was her name? She didn't have too many friends, she was like — her friends were all spaced out in different places — um, to get back. That's not a valuable list. I'll only get one more name off it.

Now, people I knew through my sister — hm — I didn't know them very well, they were just acquaintances, there's Leanne, and don't even remember his name, and let's see, don't remember her name. I'm re — I'm remembering now people, uh, who were friends of my sister's whose names I've forgotten, but who — or who I don't remember right now, but who I can remember situations where they were at — and what they looked like partially — uh — Oh, wow, OK, I just lo — located a storehouse of people. There was an afterschool thing where I used to go all the time, and there was lots of people there, and I have a whole building full of people, but I can't remember a lot of those names. There's Ruth Bower, Susan Younger, Sue Cairns — oh, wow, Jeff Andrews, Bill Jacobsen, I just located a whole another group of people — whew (laugh) wow — um —

The subject who kept recalling more names with each attempt also produced more false constructions or fabrications. Many times the fabrication was the name of an actual person, but from a different class or different part of the woman's life. A substantial number of the names people remembered were fabrications. In this study, by the tenth hour of recall almost half of the newly generated names were false ones.

The young woman whose recall was graphed remembered about 220 names out of a possible 600, after ten hours of trying. Does this mean that after spending three or four years in high school, we have information in memory on only a third of our classmates? Probably not. In this study the young woman was asked to recall the names of her classmates. In other studies names (and also faces) have been presented to people and they are asked to indicate whether or not they recognize these people. Recognition is easier than recall, and when people are asked to recognize, rather than recall, they typically show very good memory for their high school classmates. Even people who had left high school more than forty years before and were tested when they were in their sixties could identify about three-quarters of their classmates.

In sum, then, people seem to be able to remember classmates reasonably well. They generally accomplish this by first thinking of a setting or context, and then "seeing" their friends in that setting. But one must still be cautious, for memory of the good old days from high school can become clouded with fabrications.

Remembering Ourselves

Mr. Eben Frost grew up in a poor family in Vermont; the annual income barely scratched a thousand dollars. As a young boy he worked all summer on his parents' dairy farm, and in the winter would walk three miles to a two-room schoolhouse. He didn't like his life very much and longed for one in which he could talk to people. By the time he was ten years old, he planned to leave the family farm. He dreamed he would somehow go to college, and then to Harvard Law School — which is exactly what happened to him.

While at Harvard, Frost found himself becoming part of a long-term study of how people adapt to life. When he first met the psychiatrist who interviewed him, along with many other study participants, he presented himself as "a charming, warm, happy, outgoing man who was terribly interested in people."[6] He was indeed a good-looking man who conveyed a rich sense of humor. But he had to be pressed to talk about any emotionally conflicted areas, and even then, like a balky horse, his manner became uncooperative and abrupt. He liked to concentrate on the happy parts of his life. He remembered himself as being a helpful child, and that he had a great ability to make friends. He thought of himself as being particularly self-sufficient, saying so quite explicitly: "I'm so self-sufficient, or something, that I actually don't have any rough spots." At twenty-five, Frost said, "I'm a very easygoing character." And twenty years later, he said, "I'm the most reasonable of men."

The psychiatrist still tried to get Frost to recognize and admit to some of his problems. Even repeated queries about marital problems seemed to get nowhere. On one occasion, Frost wrote: "Only the stupid or the liars will say 'none,' but that is my answer." When his father died, Frost wrote: "Some people pretend that death doesn't exist and use deliberate self-delusion. Going back to the funeral was something that had to be done . . . but there was no point in carrying on." Throughout it all, he kept any unhappiness inside of him.

Is Frost unusual? Is he psychologically unhealthy? Although he may not know himself completely accurately, it turns out that his style of coping with life's problems is a mature and healthy one. Furthermore, his tendency to remember the good things about himself, and forget the bad, is common to most of us.

"I'm Better than Average"

My friend Sylvia thinks she is a better-than-average private investigator; Linda thinks she is a better-than-average business woman; Jim is a better-than-average doctor. Believing ourselves to be better than average in most ways is simply human nature. As William Saroyan put it: "Every man is a good man in a bad world — as he himself knows."

Many studies show that we perceive and remember ourselves in a way that it is more favorable than the way we probably are. A recent article entitled "Can We All Be Better than Average?" talks about the work of French psychologist Jean-Paul Codol, who conducted twenty experiments with people ranging in age from adolescence to adulthood.[7] In one of his studies, each person in a group of four gave three estimates of the length of a rod. After all the estimates were in, the experimenter measured the rod and announced its correct length. Later on, all of the participants were asked to rate how well they thought they had done. It turned out that people tended to remember themselves as being at or near the top of their group no matter how good or poor their performance. In other studies, people were asked to rate themselves on such traits as honesty or creativity. The more people admired a particular trait, such as honesty, the more likely they were to see themselves as more honest than other people.

It is easy to demonstrate the self-serving bias in memory. Ask some friends or neighbors to compare themselves with others on a variety of socially desirable traits like creativity. "What percentage of other people in our group are more creative (or honest or sympathetic or friendly) than you are?" The percentage given is usually a modest one. The bias to remember ourselves positively is quite strong with attitudes and character traits, such as honesty or considerateness, that tend to be somewhat subjective. But it even occurs with more objective matters such as a person's income or height.

People know they aren't perfect. But they tend to explain away their imperfection while hanging on to their good side. If we do something positive, it is because of some innate trait or disposition that we possess. "I donated my time for volunteer work at the local hospital because I'm a considerate person." Conversely, if we do anything nasty, it is because of some environmental factor that was beyond our control. "I yelled at you because you were acting ridiculous." Similarly, when positive things happen to us, we take credit, but when negative things happen, we shove off the blame. "I won that game of tennis because my backhand is really superb." "I lost the game of Scrabble because I got a Q and a Z and an X and there was nothing anyone could do with them."

Memory has a superiority complex. We have a tendency to think we knew all along how a given situation would turn out, despite the fact that in many cases the outcome was totally unexpected. This has been dubbed the "knew-it-all-along" effect.[8] In one study, subjects read a description of a historical or clinical event for which four possible outcomes were provided. One of the passages that was used is about a patient named George who was undergoing psychotherapy.

1) George was a very hostile boy of 28, 2) who was exceptionally bright, and 3) who managed to keep a high

school teaching job in spite of the fact that he had sexual relations with several of his own pupils. 4) He was highly promiscuous and would commonly pick up a young boy for the night, 5) blackmail or physically force him to do things that the boy hardly wanted to do, and then laugh at his distress, and sometimes even beat him up before letting him go. 6) He liked his rough and tumble "gay" life, and 7) only came to therapy because he got in trouble with the police, who forced him to come while he was on probation. 8) At first, George refused to do any work at psychotherapy, 9) as he was only waiting for his probationary term to end, and looked forward to returning to his old pattern of homosexuality. 10) The therapist kept actively trying to show him, however, that he was acting like an idiot and that, by spending his whole life trying to put other people down, he was actually achieving little pleasure for himself and was seriously defeating his own end.[9]

After reading the passage, the subjects were offered four possible outcomes: 1) continued therapy; no improvement; 2) continued therapy; improvement; 3) terminated therapy; no improvement; 4) terminated therapy; improvement. They were then asked, "In the light of the information appearing in the passage, what was the probability of occurrence of each of the four possible outcomes?" Each subject assigned a probability value to the outcomes, the sum of which had to equal 100 percent.

People tended to feel that the most likely outcome was that George terminated therapy with no improvement. It had an average probability of almost 40 percent. That George would terminate therapy with some improvement was felt to be the least likely outcome, with a probability of about 6 percent.

Other subjects in the experiment were given a piece of outcome information; for example, some were told that George continued therapy and improved, but then were asked to ignore this information and to indicate how they would have responded if they had not known the outcome. Whatever outcome they heard, the subjects were asked to ignore it and give their subjective probabilities for the four possible outcomes.

Subjects who were told that a particular outcome occurred tended to think that this outcome was much more likely to begin with. For example, when given no outcome information, subjects predicted a 39 percent chance of therapy terminating with no improvement; but when told that this had actually happened, subjects predicted a 50 percent chance of it happening. When given no outcome information, subjects predicted a 6 percent chance of therapy terminating with an improvement; but when given the information that this happened and told to ignore it, subjects felt this outcome was much more likely — now 12 percent.

These findings indicate that telling people an event has occurred causes them to believe they knew all along it was going to happen. People generally underestimate the effect that information about the outcome of an event has on their perceptions.

This same sort of intellectual conceit can be found with other sorts of materials, such as general knowledge questions taken from almanacs and encyclopedias. In one case people were asked simple questions that had two alternative answers, one of which was correct. For example, "Absinthe is: a) a precious stone, or b) a liquor." As before, for each item some subjects simply assigned a probability of being correct (between 0 and 100 percent) to the alternatives, and other subjects were given the correct answer and were then asked to respond as they would have had they not been told what the answer was. The questions covered a wide variety of content areas, such as history, music, geography, nature, and literature. The results were clear. For nearly all of the items, the subjects who were given the correct answer and told to ignore it assigned probabilities to the correct alternatives that were from 10 to 25 percent higher than the probabilities assigned by the uninformed subjects.

Why does this happen? It happens because, when a person hears an answer to a question such as "How did George's therapy turn out?" or "What is absinthe?" the answer is integrated with whatever else they knew about the topic, in order to create a coherent whole out of all relevant knowledge. Sometimes integration involves reinterpreting previously held information to make sense out of it in light of the new answer. When we hear that George stopped therapy with no improvement, we concentrate and emphasize and perhaps even exaggerate his hostility or his patterns of antisocial behavior. When asked to ignore the outcome, the aspects of the situation that are consistent with that outcome still remain salient. These processes are so natural that people do not appreciate the effect that hearing the answer had on their perceptions. For this reason, they overestimate how obvious the correct answer would be before its correctness was indicated. Thus, we rarely feel surprised by how things turn out. "I knew that Nixon would resign office long before he did." "I knew that Jane Fonda would win the Academy Award as soon as I saw that movie." The knew-it-all-along effect is at work here.

The superiority complex rears its head in many other ways. For example, people who work together on a task tend to overestimate their contribution to the task. People who engage in conversation tend to overestimate how much they contributed to the conversation. Married couples tend to overestimate the extent of their responsibility for household chores.

The married-couples study was conducted by knocking on apartment doors and asking people if they would answer a few questions.[10] One question asked husband and wife, separately, to estimate the extent of their responsibility for each of twenty activities, such as making breakfast, cleaning dishes, shopping for groceries, and so on. The results showed a strong egocentric bias.

Why do these biases occur? When people have to estimate how much they contributed, they presumably first attempt to recall the contributions that each person made.

Some aspects of the interaction are easier to recall than others. A person may simply recall a greater proportion of his or her own contributions than other people would. People have a tendency to use information that is readily available to them. Thus, if a person's own inputs are more readily available, come to mind more easily, individuals would be likely to claim more responsibility for a joint product than another person would attribute to them.

Certain processes have been identified that may be operating to increase the availability of one's own contributions. First, we may be selective about the information that we store. Our own thoughts — perhaps about what we plan to say next — and actions may distract us from paying attention to the contributions of others. We may think more about our own contributions than we do about others.

A second reason we may overestimate our own contribution is that we deliberately or even unconsciously recall our own contributions over the contributions of someone else. A third reason is that we are honestly unaware of the amount of time and effort someone else has contributed. And finally, there are undoubtedly motivational factors that come into play. A person's sense of self-esteem may be enhanced by focusing on, or weighing more heavily, his own contribution. We may dwell on our own effort because it makes us feel good.

Whatever the explanation, the research indicates a strong prevalence of self-centered biases in our memories of ourselves. In everyday life, these egocentric tendencies may not be that important in cases where no one cares about the explicit allocation of responsibility. However, when people do care, there is a great potential for dissension. People don't realize that their differences in judgment arise from honest evaluation of information that is differentially available. If they did, they would be less likely to feel as if they were underappreciated and would consequently be much less frustrated.

"I Was Better than Ever"

In addition to a superiority complex when it comes to remembering how much we contributed to some joint endeavor, our egocentric memory has a way of making us think of ourselves in a gradually more and more favorable light. People remember themselves as having held a higher level of job, received higher pay for work, purchased fewer alcoholic beverages, contributed more to charity, taken more airplane trips, and raised smarter-than-average children.[11]

In one study, interviewers talked to more than nine hundred people from a single community.[12] People were asked questions about themselves and their past, and their answers were checked with a number of objective sources. On almost every topic, significant differences were found between the answers people gave about themselves and those obtained from the records of appropriate agencies. Some examples are reported in the accompanying table.

One of the best surveys designed specifically for the purpose of measuring against official records the relative

Subject	*People giving inaccurate reports* (percent)
Contributions to Community Chest	40
Voting and registration	25
Age	17
Ownership of library card	10
Ownership of driver's license	10
Home ownership	4
Auto ownership	3
Possession of telephone	2

Inaccurate self-reports (After Parry and Crossley, 1950)

accuracy of people's memories on a range of issues is the Denver Validity Survey. In the 1949 Denver study, almost one thousand interviews were conducted with people of all ages and backgrounds, both male and female. The survey covered both attitudes and behavior related to issues of local concern. Neither the interviewers nor the respondents knew that the accuracy of the responses would be checked. The chief concern here, then, is for the kinds of inaccuracies that occur.

Some of the results are shown opposite. People tended to be fairly accurate on some kinds of items — whether they had a telephone in their home, whether they owned an automobile, how old they were. These are all issues related to the present rather than the past, and thus should prove less of a strain on the respondent's memory than the recall of other kinds of items.

Remembering whether you voted in a particular election, or whether you contributed to a particular charity, are not remembered very accurately. People tend to exaggerate their answers in a prestige-enhancing direction. They are more likely to (mis)remember that they did vote, and more likely to "recall" having given to a Community Chest drive.

We can say a bit more about the errors people make. People who ordinarily vote in elections are more likely to think that they voted in a specific election. Also, in cases in which a high proportion of people typically perform a certain civic duty like voting or giving to charity, any given individual is more tempted to exaggerate his performance than if only a small percentage of people are known to perform this prestige behavior.

In sum, then, the findings clearly showed that if a question permits a person to misinterpret or reconstruct his memories so he can give a response that is more favorable, then he will. People tend to rewrite history more in line with what they think they ought to have done than with what they actually did.

Take another example. In 1964, personal interviews were conducted with over eighteen hundred men fifty years of age

(percent)

	Correct	Exaggerated	Under-reported	Other	Actually performed the behavior
Telephone in household	98	1	1	0	85
Ownership of automobile	94	3	0	3	59
Age by driver's license record	92	4	4	0	—
Valid library card	87	9	2	2	13
Voted in 1948 presidential election	86	13	1	0	61
Voted in 1944 presidential election	73	23	2	2	38
Voted in May 1947 mayoralty election	70	28	1	1	36
Contributed to Community Chest in 1948 drive	56	34	0	10	25

The Denver validity survey (After Calahan, 1968–1969)

or older in towns and small cities of Iowa to provide bench-mark data. Ten years later, all who could be located were interviewed again (about thirteen hundred people). In 1974, a set of questions was asked to get the participants to recall their situations and attitudes in 1964.

Again, people were fairly accurate on a few of the items, but inaccurate on many others. One question asked whether the participant had a will. Almost 90 percent gave the same response in 1974 as they had given ten years earlier. One area that was notoriously inaccurate was income. In 1964, indi-viduals were asked to identify their 1964 yearly family in-come, and were also asked which would have been more valued by them — recreation, comfort, friends, or work. On each question about 40 percent of the respondents gave the same answer in 1964 and 1974. It is of interest that most of the persons (72 percent) with inconsistent responses on the income question recalled a higher income than had been re-ported in 1964. For some individuals, this difference was quite extreme. Also, people "remembered" a much stronger work orientation than actually existed. Seventy percent of those who gave inconsistent responses about their earlier values recalled work as the most important value in their lives, but previously had identified either recreation, comfort, or friends as of greater importance. Finally, two-thirds recalled that they had worked more weeks in 1964 than they had reported when previously questioned.

Thus, even for a question as straightforward as whether individuals had a will, one out of every eight provided discrep-ant responses. The situation is worse with other items that have a socially desirable side to them. "In most areas, recall responses presented respondents in a more favorable light than did information obtained in the initial interview." Dis-tortions frequently occur, especially when reality has not been repeatedly reinforced.

What we're left with, then, is a relatively positive picture of ourselves. Most people around us are perceived as being less smart, less considerate, less tolerant, less likely to give to charity. We even believe that the people in our group are likely to die sooner than we are. One psychologist found that college students view themselves as likely to live much longer than their actuarially predicted age of death. One is reminded of the man who told his wife, "If one of us should die first, I think I would go live in Paris."

This tendency to remember things more favorably than perhaps they actually were even extends to remembering our vacations. Meltzer asked college students to describe their Christmas vacation experiences. The students listed their experiences and also indicated whether the experiences were pleasant, unpleasant, or indifferent. Presumably, having a great time waterskiing constitutes a pleasant experience while getting stung by a wasp would be unpleasant for most people. Six weeks later, the students were unexpectedly asked to repeat the listing they had done immediately after returning from vacation. Not only did they list more pleasant than unpleasant memories on the day of their return, but after six weeks the predominance of pleasant over unpleasant memories increased even further.

Why do people remember themselves in a better light? Social norms have a powerful influence on a person's self-image. Cognitive dissonance can lead to a rather consistent distortion of memory in order to reinforce continued perception of oneself as a good citizen. It is possible that people exaggerate, in part, to consciously try to impress the interviewer, but it is generally believed that the major reason that we distort the truth is to enhance our own self-esteem. If cognitive distortion occurs so that our self-image is enhanced, this has important implications for how one person should go about trying to "get at the truth" from another person. All the good rapport and persistent probing may not work. What is needed is to frame the issue so that the person who is responding is unlikely to perceive a certain answer as being especially threatening to his or her self-image. But it may not always be possible to find out the truth about someone's past — not so much because people do not want to tell the truth to others,

Larger than Life

Over the years I have observed a curious phenomenon about one of my closest friends. It has happened so many times that I cannot doubt that there is something to it. It happens in this sort of situation. My friend will run into someone who hasn't seen her for some time, perhaps months or even years, and that person will remark something to the effect: "My God, you've lost weight." Now she's been an even 125 pounds for the last fifteen years; she hasn't gained, she hasn't lost. Why is it, then, that people see her in their memories as being fatter than she apparently is?

There are several possible explanations for the fat memory phenomenon. One is that she actually has lost weight but is not aware of it. This seems unlikely. A more likely possibility is related to the shift in memory toward seeing oneself in a more favorable light. One way to see ourselves more favorably is to see others less favorably. Perhaps the mental image that people have of her gradually shifts to make her fatter than she is. This may help some people think of themselves as "thinner than average," and consequently help their self-image.

Another reason why people continually think of her in their memories as being of greater dimension than she really is may have to do with her effective personality and successful career. Their mental image of her grew "larger than life" due to their nonvisual perceptions.

but because they sometimes cannot tell the truth to themselves.

A healthy distrust of one's memory, and of memory in general, is not a bad idea. When all is said and done, memory is selective; the memory machine is selective about what gets in and selective about how it changes over time. This may be adaptive in many ways. Why should we cling tightly to those memories that disturb us and spoil our lives? Life might become so much more pleasant if it is not marred by our memory of past ills, sufferings, and grievances. What good does it do for my friend Diana to remember clearly all the ways an old beau has mistreated her? We seem to have been purposely constructed with a mechanism for erasing the tape of our memory, or at least bending the memory tape, so that we can live and function without being haunted by the past. Accurate memory, in some instances, would simply get in the way. Now, knowing this, others can — if they so wish — take advantage of us. Advertisers and politicians, for example, can bend memory to their advantage. In doing so, they are simply tampering with a system that serves us well in some ways but occasionally does us in.

8
The Power
of Suggestion

As we make our way around the world, we are constantly bombarded with a steady stream of information. It comes to us from reading newspapers, engaging in conversations, watching television, going to the supermarket, going to the office. No matter what the activity, our minds are continually soaking up a colossal number of details that they somehow integrate into what feels like a consistent memory. Because memory is working at every waking moment, the potential is there, in each of these situations, for distortions to creep in. Being aware of the dangers can make for a more truthful life.

Advertising and Memory

No matter what brand of toothpaste, deodorant, or coffee a person uses, what is more interesting is how that person came to pick that particular brand. Most people will say they use a particular product because their parents did, or because a friend recommended it, but they generally won't say that they were convinced by an advertisement. We don't like to think that we are influenced by advertisements because we have a need to believe that our opinions are derived rationally. We like to think that we have given the issue some thought, and then arrived at a decision. But in many instances unconscious forces influence the way in which we make up our minds. One of the most powerful of these outside forces is advertising, and much of what we experience is designed to take account of the malleable nature of memory.

The average American probably comes across over a thousand different advertisements every day. The onslaught comes from radio and television, books and magazines, billboards and neon signs, and even from the shelves of supermarkets. Billions of dollars are spent each year getting just the right message across.

Curiously, despite vigorous attempts to be independent minded, people tend to believe what advertisers tell them. What is perhaps more dangerous, however, is that people also believe and remember things that advertisers do not tell them, things favorable to a product that can be inferred from the content of an ad only by making illogical or invalid inferences. For instance, an ad for Masterpiece cigarettes pointed out that this brand offered certain pipe tobaccos for the first time in a cigarette and said they were distinguished tobaccos. Subjects later "remembered" the ad saying something like "Pipe tobacco is as good as any tobacco for use in cigarettes." In other words, people made the illogical inference and then remembered the inference as if it were actually asserted in the ad. Similarly an ad for AC spark plugs claimed, "We make the only spark plug with four green ribs." This was accompanied by a huge illustration of the product, along with the statement "That's so you'll know it at a glance. . . ." Thus, the green ribs were for identification; nothing more was claimed. Subjects later reported as part of the ad's content the illogical inference that "green ribs are an important feature of good spark plugs."[1]

Pragmatic Implications

These invalid inferences have been called "pragmatic implications." A pragmatic implication is simply a remark that leads the hearer to expect something neither explicitly stated nor necessarily logically implied in a sentence. For example, the sentence "John pounded the nail" pragmatically implies that John was using a hammer. The sentence says nothing about a hammer; John could have been using his shoe. Thus, the sentence does not logically imply the use of a hammer, but most people will infer that this was the object that was used. "The fugitive was able to leave the country" leads people to think he left. But it doesn't say this, and he may not have left. Similarly the statement "The karate champion hit the cement block" pragmatically implies "The karate champion broke the cement block." The statement didn't say anything about the cement block breaking, but people tend to infer that this happened, and later on they actually misremember the statement, thinking that they actually heard what was only inferred by them.

Pragmatic implications are very different from logical implications. A logical implication exists when some idea is necessarily implied by an utterance. For example, the statement "John forced Bill to rob the bank" logically implies that Bill actually did rob the bank. In these cases, there is no problem if a person is led to make the inference upon hearing the sentence. With pragmatic implications, on the other hand, people will be misled.

Being able to distinguish between what is definitely asserted and what is pragmatically implied becomes critical in advertising. Although the question of what constitutes deception in advertising is controversial, one cannot make false assertions about a product without being liable for misrepresentation. Making false pragmatic implications about the product, however, leaves one considerably less vulnerable. Numerous studies show that people remember implied material as if it were asserted, and fraudulent advertisers may be able to use this technique to have their intended effect without subjecting themselves to prosecution. The potential landmark case is the one against Warner-Lambert, makers of Listerine Antiseptic (a mouthwash), for advertising by pragmatically implying false claims, which had created a "lingering false belief." The particular Listerine commercial in question was (in part):

> "Wouldn't it be great," asks the mother, "if you could make him coldproof? Well, you can't. Nothing can do that. [Boy sneezes.] But there is something that you can do that may help. Have him gargle with Listerine Antiseptic. Listerine can't promise to keep him cold-free, but it may help him fight off colds. During the cold-catching season, have him gargle twice a day with full-strength Listerine. Watch his diet, see that he gets plenty of sleep, and there's a good chance he'll have fewer colds, milder colds this year."

Some psychologists presented this commercial to subjects, changing only the product name to "Gargoil." After hearing the commercial, all of the subjects in the study thought that they heard the ad say, "Gargling with Gargoil Antiseptic helps prevent colds." Despite the disclaimers and hedges in the advertisement itself, such as "you can't" and "can't promise" and "a good chance," people made the pragmatic inference that the product would prevent colds, and they subsequently (mis)remembered that the commercial had actually told them this fact.[2]

Later work looked to see whether warning people about the problem of pragmatic implication would help make them less susceptible to the danger. Subjects heard tape recorded commercials that either directly asserted or pragmatically implied some claim about some fictional products. For many of the commercials, subjects could not distinguish between asserted and pragmatically implied claims. Warning them about pragmatic implications had very little effect.

There is something the poor consumer can do to combat the deceptive pragmatic implication. Use something called the *but not* test. If one sentence pragmatically implies another, negating the implication and conjoining the two sentences with *but* produces an acceptable sentence, as in these sentences:

The fugitive was able to leave the country, *but* he did not leave.

The karate champion hit the cement block, *but* he did not break it.

The *but* in these sentences indicates a denial of an expectation, but not a contradiction. A contradiction is produced, on the other hand, if the same test is tried with logical implication. The next two sentences are clearly unacceptable, because they state logical contradictions:

The fugitive was forced to leave the country, *but* he refused.

The karate champion broke the cement block, *but* it did not break.

Thus, the *but not* test can be used to weed the pragmatic implications out of commercials. An ad for Mazda's Cosmo announces, "EPA mileage tests say the five-speed manual transmission Cosmo gets twenty-nine miles per gallon on the highway, eighteen miles per gallon in the city." The word *say* in this ad implies but does not assert that a Cosmo will get the mileage indicated. With the *but not* test, the ad becomes: "EPA mileage tests say the . . . Cosmo gets twenty-nine miles per gallon on the highway . . . *but* the Cosmo may *not* actually get this many miles to the gallon."

In their strong ability to cause people to infer and then remember things that are not stated, pragmatic implications are very powerful devices. The reason they work is that the actual linguistic message to a person is only one of several factors that contribute to what a person will remember about the message. The listener's knowledge of the world is also important, and this cognitive contribution can have powerful effects. The fact that people will go beyond the information given to them, that they will draw inferences not explicitly stated in some message, has been known for some time. People integrate information from the message, from their general knowledge, and from their inferences, or they construct a memory for something that was never experienced in quite that way.

One situation in which these inferences are particularly likely is when a person is presented with separate parts of an idea and must connect them in order for them to make sense. Thus a person who hears "A burning cigarette was carelessly discarded. The fire destroyed many acres of virgin forest" will then infer, "A discarded cigarette started a fire," which serves as the missing link between the discarded cigarette and the fire. People will spontaneously supply these connections from their knowledge of the world. Because of the tendency for people to do this, certain special messages can be communicated through pragmatic implication; certain secondary communication goals can be achieved in this way, just as would be the case if somebody were to ask a woman, "When did you stop browbeating your husband?" thereby implying that she had in fact been browbeating him for quite some time.[3]

Whether a pragmatic implication is "deceptive" or "unfair" to consumers is a question that has caused the Federal Trade Commission a degree of unease. There is, after all, the question of the consumer's complicity in his or her own deception. When a consumer comes away from an ad with a false belief, who is responsible? Is the advertiser to be penalized for this consequence, or is it to be viewed as the consumer's tough luck? In the 1950s and early 1960s, the FTC found itself entangled in literalistic disputes over the meanings of words in ads. While it currently is attempting to avoid a kind of nit-picking, it now tends to look at the total impression generated by an ad, rejecting literal truth as a defense if that impression is false. The FTC is beginning to realize that it cannot allow an advertiser to make a claim that can be interpreted in more than one way, if one of those interpretations is likely to mislead substantial numbers of people. It is beginning to rule as inappropriate any claims made through pragmatic implication.

In terms of sheer memory for advertisements, as opposed to distortions that can occur, many studies have been conducted. Social scientists have tried to determine how many times a product name ought to be mentioned in order to optimize its chances of being recalled. They've also tried to discover if it is better to have a famous movie star push a new brand of toothpaste or an ordinary-looking character. The *Journal of Advertising Research* and the *Journal of Consumer Research* are filled with such studies. Sometimes the results are obvious, but other times they are not obvious at all.

For example, two researchers recently wondered whether it was a good idea for ads to show parts of a nude female form.[4] They reasoned that, while this showing might capture people's overall attention, it can also distract attention from the advertised product. To find out what the impact actually was on people, the researchers performed a simple study.

The subjects, 180 male business students, were shown slides of fifteen different experimental ads. Each ad contained a picture of a fictional brand of such products as tires, watches, cosmetics, or stereo sets. As brand names, the researchers picked words without familiar connotations: Bardo, Vardel, Papin & Marin. Along with each ad, the students also saw either a pastoral scene or a female model in various stages of nudity, ranging from a modest glimpse of the face and neck to a full frontal view.

The students looked at each ad and then later tried to recall as many of the products and their brand names as they could. The results were clear: The students recalled many more of those products and names accompanied by pastoral scenes than those illustrated with nudes. Surprisingly, memory did not vary significantly with the different degrees of nudity. (One odd result was that married men remembered significantly more products and brands than did single men. Could this mean that marriage makes people less distractible?)

The pictures that accompany an advertisement are exceedingly important not simply because they may or may not distract a consumer from the product or brand name, but for an additional reason. The human mind seems to integrate the information in the message (what is being asserted) with the information in any pictures that might be presented along with that message. Advertisers like to place their cars in front of glamorous mansions since many people will then come to think of the car as a fancy one, an elegant one, one that will bring them status and prestige. Cigarette advertisers like to set their ads in forests with flowing streams and mountains rising in the background so that people will come to associate their product with a healthy life-style. Few consumers can isolate the subject from the setting and make purchase decisions on the merit of the product alone.

Memory and Our Health

We often overlook the way information is obtained from a patient. Much as the questioning police officer can direct a witness's thoughts with a leading question, so can a doctor direct a patient's thoughts when the latter is being questioned about an ailment or disease. In a study I conducted some years ago, forty ordinary men and women were interviewed about their headaches and about headache products under the belief that they were participating in market research on these products.[5] Two of the questions were crucial. One of these asked about products other than that currently being used, in one of two wordings:

1) In terms of the total number of products, how many other products have you tried? One? Two? Three?

2) In terms of the total number of products, how many other products have you tried? One? Five? Ten?

The one-two-three people claimed to have tried an average of

3.3 other products whereas the one-five-ten people claimed an average of 5.2 other products.

Somewhat more subtly, I also asked about the frequency of headaches in one of two ways:

1) Do you get headaches frequently, and, if so, how often?

2) Do you get headaches occasionally, and, if so, how often?

People who were questioned with "frequently" reported a mean of 2.2 headaches per week, while those questioned with "occasionally" reported only .7.

This study hints at the very real possibility that a doctor may pragmatically imply, through the wording of his or her questions, information that may affect how the patient retrieves symptom occurrences and perceives his or her own physical condition. The implications in the doctor's questions join with the feedback from the sensory systems of the patient's body to be processed by the mind in interpreting the particular symptoms. It seems likely that the most accurate and useful reporting of the patient's symptoms in medical diagnosis is greatly affected by suggestions in a doctor's questions, just as the witness's memory is affected by suggestions in interrogation.

A question asked at one point in time can be answered differently from a question asked at a different time if the two questions are worded differently. A physician who bases a medical decision on an answer given at one point in time may be led into making the wrong decision. And even if medical interviewers were to ask questions of identical wording, which is rarely done, the nonverbal information that they communicate in their facial expression, gesticulation, and so on, varies from person to person and can cause bias in the way a patient answers. In addition to the way a question is worded and the different nonverbal cues, when topics are raised several times the patient will sometimes infer that the item is particularly important and occasionally that the preceding answer was somehow unacceptable and should be changed.

The physician too has biases. He or she expects certain answers to certain questions, based on knowledge of illness and disease. Doctors are motivated to make diagnoses and the closer they get to a decision, the greater is the expectation for corroborating responses. The danger here is that the doctor who is at once expecting a particular response is in a very good position to influence that response. For all these reasons, some physicians have advocated that medical histories be taken by computer.[6]

Because of the human memory's great capacity for suggestibility, another very real potential problem arises. Often doctors warn their patients, "This surgery may make you very dizzy and nauseous." Or a drug product warns: "This product may make you drowsy, so you should avoid driving an automobile." These statements are ostensibly intended to warn people about a potential side effect of some procedure or drug. In fact doctors now have a duty to disclose fully the risks, benefits, and options associated with most experimental procedures. The patients must give their informed consent. The very words *informed consent* seem to evoke the same sort of magic expectations one sees in fairy tales, where uttering magic words or performing magic deeds transforms frogs into princes. The proponents of the "tell-all" position seem to believe that once kissed by the doctrine, frog-patients will be autonomous princes. However, a new current of thinking worries that informed consent can, on the contrary, turn prince-patients into sickly frogs. In other words, the information might actually do harm to the patient.

A vast body of psychological and medical evidence indicates that the suggested information (especially when given in combination with a placebo — a mere sugar pill, for example) can cause symptoms that are truly physiologically unlikely. A compelling example comes from a Los Angeles physician who told a patient during an informed consent discussion that nausea and vomiting might occur after her operation was over. The next day she was given a drug to induce sleep, but shortly afterward the operation was cancelled. Upon awakening, the patient complained of extreme nausea and vomited continuously for twenty minutes. Then, when the patient was told that the operation had not taken place and that the drug she had been given does not produce nausea and vomiting, her retching immediately stopped.

These examples show how powerful suggestion is. Not only can suggested information be introduced into a patient's memory, but suggested unpleasant and unnecessary symptoms can actually be experienced by people. The suggested information is incorporated into the person's memory and this in turn leads to the experience of side effects. Precisely how this happens is still something of a mystery. One possibility is that the information causes people to become nervous, anxious, scared — and these emotions then lead to symptoms that would not otherwise be present. It is well known that too much anxiety is bad for people's health.

Memory and Politics

When John Kennedy was trying to decide whether to run for President in 1960, he enlisted the help of Lou Harris and his polls. Kennedy used Harris to find out how people felt about politics and religion in general, and whether he should openly confront the religious issue in particular. Harris designed some questions specifically to test the depth of religious tension:

> "Is there a tunnel being dug from Rome so that the Pope can have a secret entrance to the White House if Kennedy wins?"

> Kennedy was appalled by this question. "Lou," he asked, "how many did you poll with this one?" Harris told him: "About seven or eight hundred people." "You

don't think that's a little dangerous, that you might be planting the idea with some of these people?" Kennedy shot back. Harris replied: "Well, that's the risk."[7]

Politicians worry about language a lot. They know its power to change the way people think, what they remember, and perhaps most important, how they vote. Here too the pragmatic implication, which has the power to change people's memories, can be one of the most clever devices. Take the Nixon White House tapes on the subject of Watergate. Certain passages containing conversations were presented in evidence in the Watergate conspiracy trials of 1973–1974. It is easy to find many places where what is pragmatically implied may be very different from what is actually true. For example, Nixon says, "Nobody ever told me a damn bit of this, that Mitchell was guilty." This pragmatically implies that he did not know Mitchell was guilty. However, it could be that he was informed of this fact by some means other than being told. Similarly, when Nixon says, "And I just feel that I have to be in a position to be clean and to be forthcoming," he is only pragmatically implying that he is in fact clean and forthcoming. We can see this with the *but not* test. "And I just feel that I have to be in a position to be clean and to be forthcoming, even though I am not really clean and forthcoming." Nixon is safe since contradiction of a pragmatic implication is not real lying in the sense that contradiction of an assertion is taken to be.

Memory and the Law

In August, 1979, a Roman Catholic priest stood trial for a series of armed robberies in the state of Delaware. He had been identified by seven witnesses as the "Gentleman Bandit," so-called because of the polite, even diffident manners of the well-dressed robber. At his trial, this parade of witnesses positively identified the accused priest. Then, in a move that could have come from a television melodrama, the trial was abruptly halted when another man, Ronald Clouser, thirty-nine years old (and fourteen years younger than the tall, baldish priest), confessed to the robberies. Clouser said he had been deeply disturbed by the disintegration of his marriage and a mounting burden of debt. Police officers were convinced that Clouser had actually committed the crimes because he told them details that only the bandit himself could have known, details that had never come out either in the court or in the news media. The State Attorney General acted to drop charges against the priest, saying, "The state extends a sincere apology to Father Pagano." Tears ran across flushed cheeks as the priest left the courtroom for the last time. "I thank God," he said, "for the life He has given me." His tragic ordeal had finally ended.

Father Pagano later told news reporters that his experience had allowed him to see a weakness in the legal system; namely, that under certain circumstances memory can be fallible. Yet eyewitness testimony has an enormous impact on the outcome of a trial. Few things, outside a smoking pistol, carry as much weight with a jury as the testimony of an actual witness. The memory of witnesses is crucial not only in criminal cases but in civil cases as well — in automobile accident cases, for example, eyewitness testimony carries great weight in determining who is at fault. Implicit in the acceptance of this testimony as solid evidence is the assumption that the human mind is a precise recorder and storer of events. Unfortunately it is not. To see this, psychologists have set up elaborate experiments that simulate actual experience. In the case of eyewitness testimony we are presented with that rare moment in science when theory and experience mesh: the natural experiment. The courtroom is the perfect laboratory for the study of memory, and eyewitnesses are the perfect subjects.

By itself, eyewitness testimony can convict an accused person. When all the lineups held in England and Wales in 1973 were reviewed, the strength of the eyewitnesses' word became apparent. In 347 cases, the only evidence against the defendant was identification by one or more eyewitnesses; 74 percent of those defendants were convicted.

Several years ago I conducted an experiment in which people played the role of jurors in a criminal case. First they heard a description of a robbery-murder, then a prosecution argument, then an argument for the defense. In one version, the prosecution presented only circumstantial evidence; faced with this evidence, only 18 percent of the "jurors" found the "defendant" guilty. In a second version, the prosecution pled the exact case with one difference: There was testimony from a single eyewitness — a clerk who identified the defendant as the robber. Now 72 percent of the jurors found the defendant guilty.

The danger of eyewitness testimony is clear: Anyone in the world can be convicted of a crime he or she did not commit, or deprived of an award that is due, based solely on the evidence of a witness who convinces a jury that his memory about what he saw is correct. Eyewitness testimony is so powerful that it can sway a jury even after the testimony has been shown to be false.

People in general and jurors in particular are so ready to believe eyewitness testimony because for the most part our memories serve us reasonably well. But precise memory is rarely demanded of us. When a friend describes a vacation, we don't ask, "Are you sure your hotel room had two chairs, not three?" Or after a movie, "Are you sure Warren Beatty's hair was wavy, or was it curly?" If errors are made, they go unnoticed and uncorrected, and belief in an accurate memory is reaffirmed by default.

But precise memory suddenly becomes crucial in the event of a crime or an accident. Small details assume enormous importance. Did the assailant have a mustache, or was he clean shaven? Was the light red, or was it green? Did the car cross the center line, or did it stay on its own side? A case often rests on such fine details and these details are hard to obtain.

To be mistaken about details is not the result of a bad memory, but of the normal functioning of human memory. As we have seen, human remembering does not work like a videotape recorder or a movie camera. When a person wants to remember something he or she does not simply pluck a whole memory intact out of a "memory store." The memory is constructed from stored and available bits of information; any gaps in the information are filled in unconsciously by inferences. When these fragments are integrated and make sense, they form what we call a memory.

Still other factors affect the accurate perception, and therefore recollection, of an event. Was there violence? How much? Was it light or dark? Did the witness have any prior expectations or interests? And after information is perceived, it does not just lie passively, waiting to be recalled. As we have seen, many things happen to the witness during this phase: Time passes, the memory fades, and, more crucially, the witness may be exposed to new information that adds to or alters his memory.

When a crime occurs, the police are usually notified, and they come to the scene and begin to ask questions. "What happened?" the witness is asked. "What did he look like?" After the witness tells the police what he can, he may be asked to come to the police station to look through a set of photographs or to help the police artist produce a composite drawing of the offender. Now we are talking about a different aspect of human memory — in essence, the witness is now performing a recognition test. In a recognition test, either a single item (in this case a photograph) or a set of items is shown, and the person indicates whether he has seen any of them before.

Keep the obliging nature of witnesses in mind, and also the circumstances surrounding a criminal identification. Usually the police show the witness several photographs or a lineup. In both cases the witness looks at a set of faces to see if anyone appears familiar. Witnesses know that the culprit may not be in the set, but many believe that the police would not conduct the test unless they had a good suspect. Although witnesses try hard to identify the true criminal, when they are uncertain — or when no one exactly matching their memory appears in the lineup — they will often identify the person who best matches their recollection of the criminal.

Obviously, the composition of the lineup is crucial: how many people are in it, what they look like, what they are wearing. A lineup must be as free as possible from suggestive influences or it loses its value. If the suspect is a large, bearded man, the lineup should not include children, ladies in wheelchairs, or blind men with canes. Unless people resembling the suspect are included in the lineup, the suspect may be picked by default, not recognition.

But many lineups used in actual cases are grossly suggestive and the identifications they produce should be considered worthless. For example, a black suspect was put in a lineup where everyone else was white; a tall suspect stood beside short nonsuspects; and, in a case where the offender was known to be young, a suspect under twenty was placed in a lineup with five other people, all over forty.

But the problems do not vanish even when a uniform appearance has been achieved; suggestive information can affect the identification. If a police officer says, "Take another look at number four," or stares conspicuously at number four while the witness is trying to identify the culprit, the officer has provided information that can influence the choice. The witness begins to "fill in" his vague and fuzzy memory with the image of the person in front of him. Because of this filling-in process, a one-person lineup is especially dangerous. The image of the person presented for identification might well fuse with that of a fuzzy, fading memory for the criminal.

Still other common procedures are known to encourage mistaken identification. When the police have a suspect, they often show the witness a photo array and produce the actual lineup only if an identification is made. Almost invariably only the person identified appears both among the photos and in the lineup, and almost invariably the witness identifies the person he saw in the photos. These are called "photo-biased lineups"; the chances of a mistaken identification rise dramatically in these situations — again because of normal memory function.

Photo bias has affected the memory of "witnesses" in experiments at the University of Nebraska.[8] An hour or so after "witnesses" watched some "criminals" committing a "crime," they looked through mugshots that included some of the "criminals" they had seen. A week later, lineups were staged and the "witnesses" were asked to indicate those who had taken part in the original "crime." Eight percent of the people in the lineups were identified as criminals, yet they had neither taken part in the "crime" nor been among the mugshots. And a full 20 percent of the innocent people whose photographs had been included among the mugshots were also falsely identified. Despite the fact that none of these people had committed a crime, nor had they even before been seen in person, they were recognized from photographs and identified as criminals.

Once a witness has seen a person's photograph, that person will look familiar when he or she appears in a lineup. The witness may incorporate this familiarity into his memory of the crime and the criminal — and make a mistaken identification.

How many Father Paganos have been falsely arrested, wrongly convicted, and spent time in prison for crimes they never committed? How many accident victims have been denied compensation or how many drivers have wrongly been held responsible for injuries because of erroneous eyewitness testimony? We'll never know. When a case comes to light, there is a brief flurry of publicity, but then the issue is quietly forgotten.

In 1967 the United States Supreme Court acknowledged the problem in a landmark trilogy of cases: The constitutional issue the court considered was the practices and procedures used by the police to obtain eyewitness identifications. In each of the cases, the police had arranged a pretrial confrontation, a lineup between the eyewitnesses and the suspect-defendant, to see if the witness recognized the defendant. For example, in the case of *United States* v. *Wade*, Billy Joe Wade, arrested for robbing a bank, was identified in a lineup that took place without Wade's attorney. At Wade's trial, the Court stated that this identification process was riddled with factors that might seriously impair a fair trial and decided that when the government held a lineup in the absence of the accused's attorney, it violated the Sixth Amendment (right to counsel).

But five years after this landmark trilogy, the Supreme Court's decision in *Kirby* v. *Illinois* began to dismantle the earlier decisions. Thomas Kirby and his companion were found with recently stolen goods and the robbery victim positively identified Kirby and his companion as the thieves. When the case reached the Supreme Court, the convictions were upheld even though no attorney was present when the identification was made. The Court stated that the right to counsel was applicable only after a suspect has been officially charged with a crime. As a result, police now often delay formal charges until after a suspect has been identified by a witness, a practice that greatly increases the likelihood that innocent people will be mistakenly identified and convicted.

Despite these dangers, it would be a mistake to exclude all eyewitness testimony because very often, as in cases of rape, it is the only evidence available and is often correct. Even requiring a piece of evidence to corroborate an eyewitness identification would often mean excluding a valuable piece of information. Judges are often asked by attorneys to read a list of instructions to the jury on the dangers of eyewitness identification. But this method has not safeguarded the innocent, probably because judges tend to drone the instructions, and, as studies have shown, jurors either do not listen or do not understand them. One solution that works reasonably well is to call a psychologist to testify as an expert witness; he or she can explain how the human memory works and apply experimental findings to the case at hand. For example, I recently testified in the case of an armed robbery that ended in murder.

A pair of robbers held up a store manned by two clerks, one of whom they shot and killed. As soon as the robbers left the store, the surviving clerk hit the alarm. A security patrolman came almost immediately and reported finding the clerk in a state of shock. When asked for a description, all he could say was "Two men, one with a mustache; two men, one with a mustache."

Later at the police station, the clerk elaborated on his description: One of the robbers was a male Mexican adult, thirty-two to thirty-seven, about five feet, eight inches, 175 to 180 pounds, stocky build, black collar-length hair, unkempt. He also described the other robber, how the money was taken, what words were exchanged, and how the police were notified.

Together the clerk and the police constructed a composite drawing of the first robber. About two weeks after the incident, the clerk was shown a large set of black and white photographs. He said that one of the photos looked very similar to one of the robbers. The person in that photograph I'll call R. G. Actually there were two photos of R. G. in the set, but the clerk passed over the first. About a week later, the clerk was shown six color photographs. He thumbed through them and when he came to R. G.'s, he placed it aside; he continued looking at the other photos, then picked up R. G.'s photo and said, "This is the guy. I wouldn't forget the face."

Seven weeks after the incident, the security patrolman who had been slowly driving by the store just a few minutes before he got the call for the robbery and had noticed two Mexicans inside gave a statement to the police. When asked to look at photographs, he identified R. G. Later he admitted having seen R. G.'s photo in the newspaper.

R. G. was tried for robbery and murder. Because eyewitness identification was the sole evidence in the case, his defense attorney asked for the testimony of a psychologist and

I was called in. My testimony began with a brief discussion of the nature of human memory. I then discussed the psychological factors affecting eyewitness testimony that applied to this case:

- *The retention interval* How much time was there between the incident and the witness's recollection of that incident? Two weeks for the clerk, over seven weeks for the security patrolman.

- *Weapon focus* Both robbers carried guns, and the clerk's statement made it clear that the guns captured a good deal of his attention.

- *Cross-racial identification* Generally, people of one race are not likely to recognize individual differences among people of another race ("They all look alike"). The clerk and the security patrolman were white, the robbers were Mexican.

- *Post-event information* Before the security patrolman identified R. G., he saw a newspaper photo that could have supplemented his memory.

- *Unconscious transference* (confusing a person seen in one situation with a person actually seen in another situation) The clerk passed over the first photograph of R. G., but when he came to the second one, he identified R. G. Perhaps R. G. now looked familiar because his photograph, rather than himself, had been seen earlier.

In R. G.'s case, the jury was unable to reach a verdict. He was retried, the testimony was nearly identical, and the jurors were again unable to reach a verdict. It is difficult to know the reasons behind any jury verdict, or any single juror's opinion, but in this case there is a good chance that some members of the jury had too many questions about the validity of the identification to say with certainty R. G. was guilty.

Clearly, eyewitness identification should not be considered the solid, ironclad evidence it has been in the past. As we have seen, it is often incorrect. But because eyewitness testimony provides the perfect experiment on human memory, much can be learned from it.

According to the cliché, memory fades. In fact, however, it grows. What may fade is the initial perception, the actual experience of the events. But every time we recall an event we must reconstruct the memory, and so each time it is changed — colored by succeeding events, increased understanding, a new context, suggestions by others, other people's recollections.

All the things that alter memory fuse with experience, and we become sure that we saw or said or did what we remember. And even that initial perception of events is not "pure." What we see depends upon our expectations, how we identify or classify what we see, where we are. This point was driven home clearly in Kurosawa's film *Rashomon*. At a trial, three different people — a robber, a warrior, and his wife — told the story of a crime; each took part in the same event and each described the happenings from his or her point of view. Yet the stories were dramatically different.

9 Computerizing Memory

In many ways a computer is a good analogy to human memory. Its sytems — information processing and retrieval — parallel those of memory's, and the role of the programmer, both as a source of the information (including the possibility of misinformation) and as an influence that can be altered or improved, is much like a person's relationship to his or her memory. There are things we can do to improve our memory, just as we must realize there is the factor of malleability to be reckoned with. Later in this chapter we shall offer some of these helpful "tricks."

But it is the computer, in fact, which offers us the best and most sophisticated model of memory's malleable nature. Computers are capable of storing large amounts of data efficiently and retrieving needed information rapidly. The tasks faced by computer memories and the manner in which material is recalled from computer memory closely parallel those of human memory.

A medical data bank, for example, may store detailed

information about the course of thousands of patients. The data are organized so that a physician may type the characteristics of a new patient into the computer, and the computer will search its files, locate the most similar patients residing in those files, compute certain attributes about those patients, analyze their subsequent medical courses, and summarize this organized experience back on the computer screen. This process consists of identifying a specific memory, comparing it with other memories, and developing a sophisticated conclusion based upon previous experience, a problem frequently faced by human memory.

There are four requirements which underlie such computer magic. First, there must be a place to store the information. This may be on magnetic tape, on magnetic disk, or in a variety of other forms. Second, there has to be a way to know what is stored where. This function is served by a file structure and by one or several indexes. Third, there must be a method to get the information back out. This function is served by retrieval programs and subroutines. Fourth, there must be a method for aggregating raw data into meaningful concepts. This is accomplished by analysis programs and subroutines. Any memory system, biological or mechanical, must be designed to do these four things.

Computer hardware has evolved, for reasons which are more than coincidental, analogously to human memory. The computer has a central thinking area called "core." The core contains a relatively small amount of data at any particular time, but these data are immediately available for manipulation. Core corresponds, more or less, to the sensory store where human memory briefly holds incoming information. The newer computers have extended this area to include so-called virtual core. This memory facility resembles human short-term memory; information in residence here can be processed almost instantaneously. Human long-term memory is represented by storage of information in the computer data bank on magnetic disk. The information is very accessible, with random access to any desired item. But a well-organized index is required to locate a particular piece of information on the magnetic disk. Information that need not be accessed so quickly may be stored on magnetic tape instead of disk. The tape can serve as a back-up in case of loss of data from magnetic disk and can hold information that is not needed very often. It can provide redundancy and security for data. To find a desired piece of information on a tape, you must start at one end of the tape and run through it until you find what you want. These concepts (random access, back-up, redundancy, and security) must be a part of human memory. For example, removal of any portion of a mammalian brain does not disturb a particular memory. Thus, memory must be maintained redundantly and be backed up against loss due to injury to any set of brain cells.

An important difference exists between the short-term memory and the long-term memory of the computer. The computer stores information in core electrically. However, when information must be maintained and accessed over a long period of time, it is represented by physical configurations of chemicals upon a magnetic disk. Like the human brain, electrical forms of data storage are easy to manipulate, but are too fragile to allow for long-term use. If the electrical power to the computer goes off, or some other external influence interrupts the computer's normal functioning, information stored electrically is lost; that represented chemically remains.

Computer information is stored as "bits," simple switches which are either "on" or "off," but have no other values. A sequence of bits forms a code which can be a number, a letter, a word, or a concept. Computer languages exist to translate instructions given in human languages to the storage language of the machine. The machine language may perform binary operations, on bits. A programming language may enable communication of certain instructions; and a language of prompts designed for the naive user may allow the comprehension of commands phrased in the form of rather complicated constructions.

Human memory is likely to have many of these same features. Ultimately, information will be stored in some form of biological code that may not be binary, but must have a finite number of possible configurations which is less than the number of possible memories. At some level of human memory, routines must exist for the translation of the biologically coded information by "reading" into electrical form, and for progressive aggregation of that information into ever more complicated concepts. Human long-term memories may be represented by protein codes much like genetic information or by the physical connections between brain cells forming unique patterns, or by some other theory yet to be suggested. But the four basic operations of storage, indexing, retrieval, and analysis must be present.

Two of these computer requirements which must also exist in human memory have been neglected. First, there must be a file structure. Probably this file structure exhibits a branching structure or hierarchy. Second, there must be an index. There must be a map to what is stored where. The actual memory traces may be widely scattered for reasons of protection or security, but the index must be able to locate them and bring them together, and it must be able to do this within microseconds.

Many other features of the computer data retrieval process are of particular interest as we study human memory. For example, a retrieval program may read from a record stored on disk into core. It thus creates an electronic copy of the chemical memory, but makes no change in the original record stored on the disk. After that memory is used in core, the electronic copy is allowed to be destroyed, without any effect upon the original memory.

More frequently, however, a different option is employed after a memory is retrieved. The memory is brought from chemical storage to electronic storage, is modified to some extent in core, and then the new memory is replaced in the old file! After this operation, the original memory may no longer be accessed. In some systems it is kept for a while but not indexed, but ultimately it is entirely destroyed. This crucial system feature, without which no computer data bank could operate effectively, has close parallels in the malleability of human memory. With a finite brain, the malleable memory system is far more efficient than an inflexible one.

A final option is to retrieve a memory, manipulate the memory in core, and then store both the original version of the memory and the modified one. Thus, for example, one might store a series of memories about how one's opinions on a particular subject had shifted over the years. Again, such operations are critical for certain uses and must be part of any well-designed data retrieval system: a flexible system with finite capacity.

Some other tidbits of interest: Computer retrieval does not allow equal access to all possible pieces of information. Frequently retrieved items or high-priority items are usually kept maximally accessible. The hierarchy of storage allows the system to branch quickly to the appropriate subject, and data associated with that subject are often stored in the same position, in the same record. This suggests that human memory might depend strongly upon the quality of the organization of the hierarchy.

When a particular retrieval is performed several times, the programmer may devise a "macro," a subroutine which will perform that search automatically. Thus, a particular chain of reasoning need not be repeated every time the same problem is encountered. Programs that are called to the core area when they are needed serve to abstract the data, to organize the data, to compute, and to conclude. These programs, subroutines, and macros process the data. In human terms, we might forget a chain of reasoning but remember the conclusion; this use of a human "macro" would be more efficient but less flexible. We sometimes see this phenomenon in aging persons.

Usually more data are recalled to core than are actually used. Data are stored in units called "records," and even if one needs only a portion of the record, the entire record must be recalled. This inefficiency in the use of space is compensated by the ease of programming and file structure, just another of many trade-offs. For the human, calling up a memory of, for example, a book one has read seems to bring with it many more facts about the book than had been originally sought. Additional questions about that book can now be answered readily. Some waste, and some increased efficiency.

In a similar way, redundancy in computer files is usually good rather than bad. Sometimes enough improvement can be gained in the security of data or in the speed of access to data to justify the storage of high-priority information two or more times. The human brain almost certainly does this. The control theme of these points is that design of a computer memory system involves the balancing of one priority against another, speed versus size, for example, or available space versus competing priorities for that space. And any design decisions that are made will cause the memory system to operate better for some tasks than for others. The designer must choose which tasks to optimize.

Some of the possible parallels between computers and humans are listed on the table on page 177. The hippocampus might well be the physical location for the index file to human memory. It is activated each time a memory is sought, but activation of the hippocampus nerve cell is nonspecific as to the memory requested. When the power goes off to the computer, the equivalent of a seizure or electric shock to the human probably occurs. The electrical portion of memory, including the index, is obliterated. Long-term memory is not affected. During the period post-seizure, the index may be being reloaded electrically from back-up sources. Hippocampal seizures in particular appear to result in temporary loss of an index.

Short-term memory is represented in the computer by virtual core. Long-term storage is often held on magnetic disk in the computer. Temperature change in the computer alters the functions of the machine in ways similar to those in which drugs such as alcohol, marijuana, or LSD may affect the operation of the brain. Certain processes may be speeded or slowed, and certain short-circuits may be caused. The updating of files overnight, when the computer manager renders retrieval more efficient by organizing data acquired during the previous day for optimal retrieval, might be represented in some form of the human dreaming process.

Data bank	Human brain
Index file	Hippocampus
Power off	ECT/seizure
Reloading the index	Post-seizure period
Virtual core	Short-term memory
Disk storage	Cortex
Temperature change	Systemic drug
"Save file replace"	The malleability of memory
Updating files overnight	Dreaming

Some possible parallels

The central message of this part of the chapter is that the human brain and the computer data bank are finite resources. Models of human memory have frequently ignored constraints upon the amount of data which might be stored and retrieved. The human brain, over many ages, has increased in size, possibly because of the increased likelihood of survival afforded the organism with increased powers of mentation. But the cranial cavity is clearly a space with a finite volume. To use portions of that space to store information that will never be accessed, or to fail to include provision for pruning unneeded data from time to time, or to fail to provide for the replacement of one memory item by another, would be very poor design indeed.

Making the Most of What We Have

If the malleability of memory is a given, how are we to process the ever-expanding ocean of knowledge that comes our way? Magazines and newspapers, movies and plays — the complexities of modern life — immerse us in a flood of information. We are living in a world of information, and success functioning requires that we master a great deal of knowledge. Like a computer programmer, we are forced to design "programs" that make optimum use of our memory capacities. Most people want to know something about politics and economics, about literature and art. To do this well, we must call upon our memory.

People also want to remember names and facts. Some of the top experts on memory training have said that forgetting things can be more than just an irritant; it can also be costly for a busy person. It creates stress and takes up valuable time. An unreliable memory also hurts a person's self-confidence and peace of mind. People dodge other people at parties because they can't for the life of them remember names. When people can't recall things they have read, it affects their conversations. It can make an unfavorable impression on one's boss or a potential client.

Memory is important, no doubt about it. But given that our memories are continually subject to distortions and transformations, how can we hang on to the truth? If it is natural and normal for people's memories to become altered, is there anything that one can do?

Probably the most important thing a person can do to improve memory is learn how to pay attention. Every time you allow your attention to wander, you miss something. In my work, it is important to read a great deal; it is not uncommon for me to read an entire page of a book and then remember nothing from it. This happens because I start daydreaming and allow my attention to wander to some other matter — what I need to buy at the grocery store, where I am going on my next trip, why someone has been nasty to me. Sometimes I have to read the same material several times before it sinks in. This same thing happens to people while they are driving. Most people have had the experience of driving a few miles in a car and suddenly realizing they cannot remember anything of the scenery for the previous few minutes. Attention wanders, and memory suffers. But there is something that can be done.

Two factors affect attention and to the extent that we understand these factors we will be better able to control our attention. The first has to do with the stimuli in our environment. Some environmental stimuli force themselves on us more than others. Advertisers understand this. They use bright colors, catchy phrases, movement — all known to be grabbers of attention. Novelty gets our attention.

The second factor that affects our attention is our own interest. We have some freedom in what we choose to focus on. It is possible to focus hard on some information and effectively block out most other stimuli and thoughts.

Increased attention raises the chances that everyday information will be remembered. It is, in part, the reason why trivia whizzes — those people who seem to be able to remember the star of every movie they've ever seen or the batting average of every player on their favorite team — do so well. The trivia whizzes typically have an interest in this sort of trivia, or they wouldn't have focused their attention on it in the first place.

Once interest in a topic is strong enough, attention to that topic becomes almost automatic. Every time we hear the topic mentioned, our ears perk up. The more interest we have, the more we can learn. And the more we learn, the more interest we have. The cycle continues.

Many times, however, people must learn things that they are not overwhelmingly interested in. This can certainly be done. By paying attention to the topic under discussion, you can learn more about it. This may occur slowly at first, but as you get to know more — about football, about operas, about an individual — the easier it becomes for you to tell when people are talking about it and when you should pay attention. Once attention becomes automatic, picking up information about a topic becomes easier.

Paying attention has another benefit. Interesting information enters our memory more securely, is more resistant to distortion, and is better able to fend off potential suggestions for future malleability.

Let's say you're a tourist in New York and have just asked for directions to the Museum of Modern Art. One of the important techniques at this stage is to try to organize the information by relating it to what you already know. This forces you to think about the information to understand it better. It also makes you dredge up old information from memory and think about it again.

For getting to the Museum of Modern Art, it helps if your information source tells you of some familiar place near where you want to go — say Saks Fifth Avenue. Then you can remember the new place in relation to what you already know. (Another trick for getting back to your hotel: As you walk toward the Museum look back over your shoulder every so often so that you can see how things will look when you are on your way back. The world looks very different coming and going.)

If you hear a story about someone, or see some unusual event, it also helps to relate it to what you already know. But there is more you can do. Rehearsing the information, either aloud or to yourself, will do much to help transfer it to long-term memory where it can be retrieved later on.

Memory experts have developed a number of different tricks — called mnemonic devices — for helping people fight forgetting. Many people who suffer from what they think is a poor memory turn to these tricks, but do they really work?

Fighting Forgetting

"The horror of that moment," the King went on, "I shall never, never forget!"

"You will, though," the Queen said, "if you don't make a memorandum of it."

— Lewis Carroll

One evening the Greek poet Simonides was reciting poetry at a huge banquet given by a well-to-do nobleman. Midway through the banquet, Simonides was abruptly drawn away from the banquet by a messenger of the gods. Barely a few moments passed and the entire roof of the banquet hall collapsed, crushing all the guests. Not a single guest survived this horror. The grief-stricken relatives of the guests faced a further tragedy: The bodies of their loved ones were so mutilated that they could not be identified. How were these people to be buried properly? At first, the situation seemed to have no solution, but then Simonides discovered that the task might not be impossible. He found he could mentally picture the exact place at which each guest had been sitting, and in this way he could identify the bodies. Through this tragic experience, Simonides discovered a technique that could be used to remember all sorts of objects and ideas. He simply assigned these items fixed positions in space. This powerful method has come to be known as the "method of loci," *loci* meaning roughly "locations."

The method of loci has been discovered and successfully used by persons who are able to memorize stupefying amounts of material. One example is the newspaper reporter S, the subject of Alexander Luria's pioneering work mentioned in Chapter 1. S could visualize dozens of items that he wanted to remember by placing them along a familiar street in Moscow. When he wanted to remember the items, he would simply mentally walk along the street, "seeing" the items as he passed. He rarely made a mistake, but when he did he tended to blame it on a misperception rather than an error of memory. Once the word *egg* was one he wished to remember but instead forgot. Why? Because he had imagined it against a white wall. It completely blended into the background and he did not "see" it when he took his mental walk.

The method of loci is easy. First you memorize a series of mental snapshots, or locations that are familiar to you, a series that follows in a regular order. For example, you might think of the distinct places you pass as you walk from your house to the nearest bus stop. Or you might imagine the distinct locations you see each morning — your bed, the bathroom door, the bathroom sink, the top of the stairs, the breakfast table.

The locations will serve as pigeonholes for any items you want to learn. Say it is a shopping list of butter, eggs, hamburger, and toothpaste. First you will need to convert each item into a visual image. Then put an image of each item in a specific location on your mental snapshot. Thus, you might imagine a pound of butter sitting at the end of your bed, then some eggs on the floor in front of the bathroom door, then a hamburger in the bathroom sink, and finally toothpaste squeezed over the top step of the stairway. Think about each item in location for about five or ten seconds. Then, when you want to remember the list later, simply take a "mental walk" past the various locations and you will be able to note what you have placed in each one.

The method of loci is an example of a mnemonic device, or a memory trick. Your memory associates new items with old ones. Some new items are complex and require a good deal of effort and concentration to master, but most are relatively simple and easy to learn. These techniques allow people to remember a good deal more information than they would ordinarily be able to using rote memorizing techniques. Occasionally people are found who have exceptional abilities to memorize by rote. One example is a man dubbed V. P. by the psychologists who studied him. Before he had reached the age of five, V. P. had memorized the street map of a city of half a million people. By the time he was ten, he memorized 150 poems as part of a contest. V. P. was raised in Latvia and was schooled in a system that emphasized rote learning. It is tempting to conclude that his early training may have provided V. P. with the impetus to improve his mnemonic skills.

Most of us with ordinary memories cannot remember a lot of information by rote. But using mnemonic devices, we can remember a good deal more than we might otherwise be able to.

Another efficient way to remember a series of items is the peg word method. The first step is to learn a list of peg words that correspond to the numbers one through twenty. Here's a list that has been commonly used for the first ten numbers:

One is a bun	Six is sticks
Two is a shoe	Seven is heaven
Three is a tree	Eight is a gate
Four is a door	Nine is wine
Five is a hive	Ten is a hen

Basically, the method works by having you "hang" the items you want to remember on the pegs. Each item goes with one peg, and the two are imagined interacting with each other. Thus, if you wanted to remember the shopping list given before — butter, eggs, hamburger, toothpaste . . . — you might compose an image of butter resting between the two halves of a bun, the eggs spilling over the edge of a shoe, the hamburger lying next to a tree, then toothpaste dripping over a door. The pairs become associated in your mind. Then when you attempt to remember the list, you go through the peg words and note what object you visually placed on each peg. The pegs, like the locations in the method of loci, give you cues necessary to recover your memories.

Another technique for remembering a list is to make up a story. Weave the items into a story that ties them together. The crazier the story, the better. So, to ensure that I will be able to remember the shopping list, I might imagine that I am a cook in a local coffee shop. One day I am busy spreading butter over the sandwich bread when two people come in, both nagging each other. The man says he wants some eggs. His wife says, "It's dinner time. Wouldn't you rather have a hamburger?" He tells her no. When she presses him for an explanation, he says, "Stop nagging" and pulls out a tube of toothpaste and hits her over the head. This technique has been called the "narrative-chaining" method. It is effective for learning a single list, but its real power comes when several different lists have to be learned. In one study, people who had used narrative chaining remembered over six times as much as people who learned by ordinary rote memorization. While the method of loci and the peg word methods are just as good as narrative chaining when a single list has to be remembered, the latter method is more efficient when many lists must be remembered. This is one example of the fact that the kind of technique that works best depends upon the material to be learned.

Learning a Foreign Language

Suppose you are planning a trip to China and are nervous about the fact that you won't know the men's room from the ladies'. Or your company has just assigned you to spend six months in Mexico City and many of your customers won't know a word of English. Or perhaps you've always wanted to read certain Swedish novels in their original language. Whatever your reason, for the first time in your life you have a strong desire to master a foreign language. How much effort you have to put in depends upon whether you are trying to learn a difficult language like Chinese or an easier one like Spanish.

There are many approaches you can take. You might consider going to a commercial school such as Berlitz, the largest chain. You might plan on taking an extension course at a nearby college or university. You might try doing it on your own, either with a private tutor, or with an easy mnemonic system and a set of vocabulary cards. The mnemonic system involves essentially two steps. The first is to find a part of the foreign word that you want to remember that sounds like an English word. The Spanish *caballo*, which means "horse," is pronounced *cob-eye-yo*. Thus, *eye* can be used as the key word. The next step is to use an image to connect the key word and the English equivalent. So, you might imagine a horse kicking a giant eye, as you see below. Later on, when you are trying to remember what the word *caballo* means, you would first retrieve *eye* and then the stored image that links it to *horse*. Similarly the Spanish word *pato*, which means "duck," is pronounced *pot-o*. Thus, *pot* can be used as the key word. An image that connects the key word to the English equivalent might be a duck with a pot over its head. When asked for the meaning of *pato* you would first retrieve *pot*, and then the stored image that links it to *duck*. At first this may sound quite complicated, but studies have shown that the key word method makes learning a foreign language a lot easier.

Mental images used to associate Spanish words with corresponding English terms.
(*From* Introduction to Psychology, *7th ed., by Ernest R. Hilgard, Rita L. Atkinson, and Richard C. Atkinson. Copyright © 1979 by Harcourt Brace Jovanovich, Inc. Reproduced by permission of the publisher.)*

I'll Never Forget What's-His-Name

People commonly report having problems remembering the names of others. A face looks familiar, but the name escapes us. This problem, too, can be helped with a simple trick.

The overall problem breaks down into three subproblems: remembering the face, the name, and the connection between the two. For the first part, remembering the face, look at it carefully while focusing on some distinctive feature such as bushy eyebrows. For the second part, remembering the name, try to find some meaning in it. As in the case of foreign language, you might think about a part of the name that sounds like an English word. Finally, to remember the connection between the face and name, think of an image that links the key word and the distinctive feature in the face. If you have just been introduced to Mr. Clausen, the man with the bushy eyebrows, you might think of the English word *claws* as a key word for Clausen. Now imagine a large lobster claw tearing away at Mr. Clausen's bushy eyebrows. Now, when you see Mr. Clausen the next time, conjure up the image of the claw at his eyebrow, and the name Clausen should come to mind.

Studies have shown that this method helps the facial feature, the key word, and the name to become tightly woven together. And the result is that people with no previous practice remember many more faces when they use the method as when they do not. In one study, if a person remembered the facial feature and the key word, the chances of remembering the name were about 90 percent. Sometimes people make errors, but these are usually the result of poor association of the key word to the name. Most people who forget the key word or the facial feature will not be able to remember the name. And people who forget both the feature and the key word are unlikely to remember the name at all. The trick in using this technique is to practice being able to convert a name to some memorable key word. After that, it is easy.

Another technique for remembering people's names involves the use of an expanding pattern of rehearsal, an idea developed by Tom Landauer of Bell Laboratories and Robert Bjork of UCLA. When you are introduced to someone, repeat the name immediately. You might say something like "Betty Johnson? Hello, Betty." About ten or fifteen seconds later, look at the person and rehearse the name silently. Do this again after one minute, and then three minutes, and the name will have a very good chance of becoming lodged in your long-term memory. Part of the reason this spacing technique works is because most forgetting occurs within a very short time after you learn some new fact.

Other Memory Aids

There seems to be no doubt that the memory systems help people recall information that they could not otherwise remember. They work because they make use of principles that are well established, such as helping retrieval of information by developing a retrieval plan, and exploiting the beneficial effects of imagery on memory. They may also work because they improve a person's motivation to learn and guarantee that the material to be learned is as well organized as possible. If a person is motivated to learn, he or she will pay more attention to items that have to be remembered. If a person is asked to imagine the items, this may make the whole job more interesting, more significant, which in turn will help in the long run.

A major difficulty with many of these memory tricks is that they are largely useful for recalling simple lists such as lists of grocery items. This may help in a pinch, but in general they don't help a great deal when it comes to the kinds of memories that play a major part in everyday life. The two exceptions, of course, are the memory aids in foreign language learning, and the aids for linking names and faces. The study of memory aids is important, in part because it will undoubtedly lead to a greater understanding of how best to help those with memory problems.

Most of the mnemonic tricks that psychologists study

have made use of what we might call an "internal aid." But these turn out to be not what people typically use in everyday life. In one study conducted in England, people were interviewed about which memory aids they used and how often. They were asked about the extent to which they used internal aids (such as the method of loci, face-name associations, and others) and the extent to which they used external aids, such as shopping lists, diaries, writing on their hand, and so on. Most people claimed to use external aids such as diaries or calendars while very few ever used the internal aids advocated by memory experts such as Harry Lorayne, who has often gone on TV talk shows and reeled off the names and addresses of the studio audience. Lorayne claims he has no special gift, but that he is highly motivated and has trained himself. He insists that his techniques work because they rely on the mind's natural tendency to create associations. He shuns the external aids, like writing things on a piece of paper. "You can lose a piece of paper," he says, "but you can't lose your mind."[1] Lorayne is partly right and partly wrong. Your mind can't fall behind a desk and accidentally into a wastebasket, the way a piece of paper can. But the mind cannot hold information unfailingly. Memory is malleable; the words on a piece of paper are not. Thus, the best advice for enhancing memory is to develop both the internal and external aids.

One of the most widely discussed types of memory is "photographic" memory. Although people use this term freely, many do not know what a photographic memory actually is. The closest approximation to what we might call a photographic memory is "eidetic imagery." People with eidetic imagery can visualize a scene with almost photographic clarity. A person with eidetic imagery experiences images as if they were "out there" in space rather than as if they were inside the mind. The eyes move over a visualized scene as if it had the quality of a real perception, and the person can at the same time describe the scene in uncanny detail.

Robert A. Lovett, former U.S. Secretary of Defense, is one such person. He first became aware of his unusual ability in high school, where he excelled in foreign languages and mathematics. His memory continued to flourish during his days at Harvard Law School, where he participated in several moot court cases. Just coincidentally, the final examination in one course asked about one of the cases that he had prepared for moot court. Lovett answered the exam question by quoting the case verbatim, with case numbers and all. He was strongly suspected of cheating and confronted with this suspicion by his professor, Dean Roscoe Pound. "Mr. Lovett, you realize I must give you either an A or a zero." Lovett answered: "Would it help, Dean Pound, if I quoted the case to you now?" — which he proceeded to do, once again, line by line.

Lovett's memory, despite occasional problems of leaving him feeling his mind was cluttered, was rather exceptional. This ability is extremely rare, despite the attention it has drawn.

Malleability Revisited

It is a fact that forgetting is commonly a case of temporary rather than permanent failure. And it is precisely because of this fact that people have argued that no memory is ever completely lost. An experience leaves its mark on memory as clearly as a burglar leaves fingerprints. Yet the basic proposition that nothing a person experiences is ever lost is itself untestable. Even Freud was later forced to modify his position, albeit slightly, and he became content to say that nothing that was in the mind need ever perish. But it is quite possible, as we have seen, that things do perish. Whenever some new information is registered in memory, it is possible that the previous relevant memories are reactivated to assimilate the new information and are modified in the process.

No doubt there are good evolutionary reasons for a human being to be designed with a malleable memory. No one knows what the limits are on the amount of information that the human mind can store. But it is highly likely that beyond certain limits, the more information that is stored in memory, the longer it takes to find a particular bit of information, and the greater the chance of incorrectly storing a fact or retrieving an incorrect fact. There may therefore be sound economic reasons for discarding some information altogether, for updating memory, and for relegating less useful memories to rear dusty mental files. Only the memories that are biologically useful or that have personal value and interest need stay alive and active.

We can minimize potential distortions in important memories through a few simple techniques. Rehearsing the experience in our minds or out loud will help preserve the memory. Research has shown that people who are warned that someone may try to change their memories can better resist these influences than people who are not warned. The mechanism by which people resist is twofold: They rehearse the experience, and they better scrutinize the new information to detect inconsistencies with their already-stored memory.

The malleability of human memory represents a phenomenon that is at once perplexing and vexing. It means that our past might not be exactly as we remember it. The very nature of truth and of certainty is shaken. It is more comfortable for us to believe that somewhere within our brain, however well hidden, rests a bedrock of memory that absolutely corresponds with events that have passed. Unfortunately, we are simply not designed that way. It is time to start figuring out how to put the malleable memory to work in ways that can serve us well. Now that we are beginning to understand this phenomenon, new research may begin to tell us how to control it. It would be nice, for example, if an individual could decide whether he or she wanted to have an accurate memory versus a "rosy" memory. By controlling the inputs into memory, it should theoretically be possible to achieve what we wish. For accuracy, we need balance; for a rosy memory, we need one-sided inputs. We need not be afraid of or disquieted by the nature of our memories; we need only to make them work on our behalf.

Notes

Chapter 1

1. J. Sandulescu, "An Uncommon Friendship," *Quest*, 1979, 3, pp. 63–67.
2. B. W. Levinson, "States of Awareness During General Anaesthesia," in *Hypnosis & Psychosomatic Medicine*, ed. by J. W. Lassner (Berlin & New York: Springer-Verlag, 1967), p. 23.
3. Ibid., p. 24.

Chapter 2

1. I. Asimov, *Is Anyone There?* (Garden City, NY: Doubleday, 1967).
2. L. R. Peterson and M. J. Peterson, "Short-term Retention of Individual Verbal Items," *Journal of Experimental Psychology*, 1959, 58, pp. 193–198.
3. J. L. McGaugh and L. F. Petrinovich, "Neural Consolidation and Electroconvulsive Shock Reexamined," *Psychological Review*, 1966, 73, pp. 382–387.
4. B. R. Milner, "Amnesia Following Operation on Temporal Lobes," in *Amnesia*, ed. by C. W. N. Whitty and O. L. Zangwill (London: Butterworth, 1966).

5. P. Gould and R. White, *Mental Maps* (New York: Penguin Books, 1974).

Chapter 3

1. P. F. Drucker, "What Freud Forgot," *Human Nature*, 1979, *2*, pp. 40–47.
2. *Time*, June 25, 1979, p. 68.
3. G. W. Allport and L. J. Postman, "The Basic Psychology of Rumor," in *Readings in Social Psychology*, 3rd ed., ed. by E. E. Maccoby, T. M. Newcomb, and E. L. Hartley (New York: Holt, Rinehart & Winston, 1958).
4. S. Freud, *Psychopathology of Everyday Life* (London: Hogarth Press, 1960).
5. P. Rieff, *Freud: The Mind of the Moralist* (New York: Viking Press, 1959).
6. S. Freud, *Introductory Lectures on Psychoanalysis*, trans. by James Trachley (New York: Liveright, 1967), pp. 178–179.
7. E. F. Loftus and G. R. Loftus, "On the Permanence of Stored Information in the Human Brain," *American Psychologist*, 1980, *35*, pp. 409–420.
8. E. F. Loftus, "Leading Questions and the Eyewitness Report," *Cognitive Psychology*, 1975, *7*, pp. 560–572.
9. W. Penfield, "Consciousness, Memory and Man's Conditioned Reflexes," in *On the Biology of Learning*, ed. by K. Pribram (New York: Harcourt, Brace & World, 1969).
10. C. Blakemore, "The Unsolved Marvel of Memory," *New York Times Magazine*, Feb. 6, 1977. Reprinted in *Readings in Psychology 78/79* (Guilford, CT: Annual Editions, Dushkin Publishing Group, 1978), pp. 87–91.
11. Penfield, p. 165.
12. Ibid., p. 152.
13. Ibid., p. 154.
14. W. Penfield and P. Perot, "The Brain's Record of Auditory and Visual Experience," *Brain*, 1963, *86*, pp. 595–696.
15. Ulric Neisser, *Cognitive Psychology* (New York: Appleton-Century Croft, 1967), p. 169.
16. G. F. Mahl, A. Rothenberg, J. M. R. Delgado, and H. Hamlin, "Psychological Responses in the Human to Intracerebral Electrical Stimulation," *Psychosomatic Medicine*, 1964, *26*, pp. 337–368.
17. E. R. Hilgard, *Divided Consciousness: Multiple Controls in Human Thought and Action* (New York: Wiley, 1977); and J. V.

McConnell, *Understanding Human Behavior*, 2nd ed. (New York: Holt, Rinehart & Winston, 1977).

18. B. B. Raginsky, "Hypnotic Recall of Aircrash Cause," *International Journal of Advertising Research*, 1971, *11*, pp. 19–24.
19. D. B. Cheek and L. M. LeCron, *Clinical Hypnotherapy* (New York: Grune & Stratton, 1968).
20. *TV Guide*, Oct. 4–10, 1975, p. 34.
21. McConnell.
22. M. T. Orne, "The Mechanisms of Hypnotic Age Regression: An Experimental Study," *Journal of Abnormal and Social Psychology*, 1951, *46*, pp. 213–225.
23. *ABA Journal*, Feb. 2, 1978.
24. L. Z. Freedman, " 'Truth' Drugs," *Scientific American*, 1960, *202*, pp. 145–154.
25. M. J. Gerson and V. M. Victoroff, "Experimental Investigation into the Validity of Confessions Obtained Under Sodium Amytal Narcosis," *Clinical Psychopathology*, 1948, *9*, pp. 360–375.
26. Ibid., p. 362.
27. Freedman.

Chapter 4

1. I. M. L. Hunter, *Memory* (Baltimore: Penguin Books, 1964).
2. H. Lorayne and J. Lucas, *The Memory Book* (New York: Ballantine, 1974), p. 1.
3. J. G. Jenkins and K. M. Dallenbach, "Oblivescence During Sleep and Waking," *American Journal of Psychology*, 1924, *35*, pp. 605–612.
4. H. Minami and K. M. Dallenbach, "The Effect of Activity on Learning and Retention in the Cockroach," *American Journal of Psychology*, 1946, *59*, pp. 1–58.
5. R. Brown and D. McNeill, "The 'Tip of the Tongue' Phenomenon," *Journal of Verbal Learning and Behavior*, 1966, *5*, pp. 325–337.
6. A. D. Yarmey, "I Recognize Your Face but I Can't Remember Your Name: Further Evidence on the Tip of the Tongue Phenomenon," *Memory and Cognition*, 1973, *1*, pp. 287–290.
7. P. G. Zimbardo and F. L. Ruch, *Psychology and Life* (Glenview, IL: Scott, Foresman & Co., 1975), pp. 156–157.
8. J. G. Dunne, "On the Matter of Chappaquiddick," *New West*, Dec. 3, 1979.

9. R. S. Nickerson and M. J. Adams, "Long-term Memory for a Common Object," *Cognitive Psychology,* 1979, *11,* pp. 287–307.

Chapter 5

1. A. D. Baddeley, "Selective Attention and Performance in Dangerous Environments," *British Journal of Psychology,* 1972, *63,* pp. 537–546.
2. J. M. Siegel and E. F. Loftus, "Impact of Anxiety and Life Stress upon Eyewitness Testimony," *Bulletin of the Psychonomic Society,* 1978, *12,* pp. 479–480.
3. M. Perlberg, "Trauma at Tenerife," *Human Behavior,* April, 1979, pp. 49–50.
4. T. E. Drabeck and E. L. Quarantelli, "Scapegoats, Villains, and Disasters," *Transaction,* March, 1967, pp. 12–17.
5. G. Talland, *Disorders of Memory and Learning* (New York: Penguin Books, 1968); and O. L. Zangwill, "Amnesia and the Generic Image," *Quarterly Journal of Experimental Psychology,* 1950, *2,* pp. 7–12.
6. R. Mayeux, "Sexual Intercourse and Transient Global Amnesia," *New England Journal of Medicine,* April 12, 1979, p. 864.
7. Hilgard.
8. R. S. De Ropp, *Drugs and the Mind* (New York: Dell Publishing Co., 1976), p. 122.
9. Ben Jones and Marilyn Jones, "Alcohol and Memory Impairment in Male and Female Social Drinkers," in *Alcohol and Human Memory,* ed. by I. M. Birnbaum and E. S. Parker (Hillsdale, N. J.: Erlbaum, 1977).
10. Ibid., originally discussed in B. M. Jones, "Memory Impairment on the Ascending and Descending Limbs of the Blood Alcohol Curve," *Journal of Abnormal Psychology,* 1973, *82,* pp. 24–32.
11. E. S. Parker and E. P. Noble, "Alcohol Consumption and Cognitive Functioning in Social Drinkers," *Journal of Studies on Alcohol,* 1977, *38,* pp. 1224–1232.
12. De Ropp, p. 131.
13. O. A. Parsons and G. P. Prigatano, "Memory Functioning in Alcoholics," in Birnbaum and Parker, pp. 185–194.
14. D. W. Goodwin, "The Alcoholic Blackout and How to Prevent It," in Birnbaum and Parker, pp. 177–183.
15. L. L. Miller et al., "Marijuana: An Analysis of Storage and Retrieval Deficits in Memory with the Technique of Restricted

Reminding," *Pharmacology Biochemistry & Behavior*, 1978, 8, pp. 327–332.

16. C. F. Darley, J. R. Tinklenberg, W. T. Roth, L. E. Hollister, and R. G. Atkinson, "The Influence of Marijuana on Storage and Retrieval Processes in Memory," *Memory and Cognition*, 1973, *1*, pp. 196–200.

17. R. T. Jones, "Tetrahydrocannabinol and the Marijuana-Induced Social 'High,' or the Effects of the Mind on Marijuana," in *Marijuana: Chemistry, Pharmacology, and Patterns of Social Use, Annals of the New York Academy of Sciences*, 1971, *191*, pp. 155–165.

18. R. Carr, "What Marijuana Does (and Doesn't Do)," *Human Behavior*, January, 1978. Reprinted in *Readings in Psychology 79–80* (Guilford, CT: Dushkin Publishing Group, 1979).

Chapter 6

1. Paul Baltes and K. Warner Schaie, eds., *Lifespan Developmental Psychology: Personality and Socialization* (New York: Academic Press, 1973).

2. J. Botwinick, *Aging and Behavior*, 2nd ed. (New York: Springer Publishing Co., 1978); and F. I. M. Craik, "Age Differences in Human Memory," in *Handbook of the Psychology of Aging*, ed. by J. E. Birren and K. W. Schaie (New York: Van Nostrand & Co., 1977).

3. Botwinick.

4. J. Inglis and W. K. Caird, "Age Differences in Successive Responses to Simultaneous Stimulation," *Canadian Journal of Psychology*, 1963, *17*, pp. 98–105.

5. Craik.

6. Ibid.

7. T. Farrimond, "Retention and Recall: Incidental Learning of Visual and Auditory Material," *Journal of Genetic Psychology*, 1968, *113*, pp. 155–165.

8. D. Shakow, M. B. Dolkart, and R. Goldman, "The Memory Function in Psychoses of the Aged," *Diseases of the Nervous System*, 1941, *2*, pp. 43–48.

9. E. K. Warrington and M. Silberstein, "A Questionnaire Technique for Investigating Very Long-term Memory," *Quarterly Journal of Experimental Psychology*, 1970, *22*, pp. 508–512.

10. H. P. Bahrick, P. O. Bahrick, and R. P. Wittlinger, "Those Unforgettable High School Days," *Psychology Today*, December, 1974, pp. 50–56.

11. P. B. Baltes, H. W. Reese, and J. R. Nesselroade, *Life-Span Developmental Psychology: Introduction to Research Methods* (Monterey, CA: Brooks/Cole, 1977).

Chapter 7

1. G. Wolff, "The Guilt of Sons, the Lies of Fathers," *Esquire*, July 3–19, 1979, pp. 23–24.
2. J. Piaget, *Plays, Dreams and Imitation in Childhood* (New York: Norton, 1962).
3. P. H. Lindsay and D. A. Norman, *Human Information Processing: An Introduction to Psychology* (New York: Academic Press, 1972).
4. R. Brown and J. Kulik, "Flashbulb Memories," *Cognition*, 1977, 5, pp. 73–99.
5. M. Linton, "I Remember It Well," *Psychology Today*, July, 1979, pp. 81–86.
6. G. E. Vaillant, *Adaptation to Life* (Boston: Little, Brown, 1977).
7. D. G. Myers and J. Ridl, "Can We All Be Better than Average?" *Psychology Today*, 1979, 13, pp. 89–98.
8. B. Fischhoff, "Hindsight-Foresight: The Effect of Outcome Knowledge on Judgment Under Uncertainty," *Journal of Experimental Psychology: Human Perception and Performance*, 1975, 1, pp. 288–299.
9. A. Ellis, "Psychosexual and Marital Problems," in *An Introduction to Clinical Psychology*, ed. by L. A. Berg and L. A. Pennington (Ronald Press, 1967), p. 204.
10. M. Ross and F. Sicoly, "Egocentric Biases in Availability and Attribution," *Journal of Personality and Social Psychology*, 1979, 37, pp. 322–336.
11. C. F. Cannell and R. L. Kahn, "Interviewing," in *The Handbook of Social Psychology*, 2nd ed., ed. by G. Lindzey and E. Aronson, Vol. 11: Research Methods (Reading, MA: Addison-Wesley, 1968).
12. H. Parry and H. Crossley, "Validity of Responses to Survey Questions," *Public Opinion Quarterly*, 1950, 14, pp. 61–80.

Chapter 8

1. I. Preston and S. E. Scharbach, "Advertising: More than Meets the Eye?" *Journal of Advertising Research*, 1971, 11, pp. 19–24.
2. R. J. Harris and G. E. Monaco, "Psychology of Pragmatic Implication: Information Processing Between the Lines," *Journal of Experimental Psychology: General*, 1978, 107, pp. 1–22.

3. T. Murray and E. F. Loftus, "The Constructive Mind of the Consumer," unpublished manuscript, University of Washington, 1978.

4. M. W. Alexander and B. Judd, *Journal of Advertising Research, 18,* cited in *Psychology Today,* June, 1979, p. 36.

5. Loftus, 1975.

6. W. V. Slack et al., "A Computer-Based Medical History System," *New England Journal of Medicine,* 1966, *274,* pp. 194–198.

7. D. Halberstam, *The Powers That Be* (New York: Knopf, 1979).

8. E. Brown, K. Deffenbacher, and W. Sturgill, "Memory for Faces and the Circumstances of Encounter," *Journal of Applied Psychology,* 1977, *62,* pp. 311–318.

Chapter 9

1. M. Witty, "Memory: An Article You'll Never Forget," *Quest/ 80,* January, 1980, pp. 97–98.

Index